Advance praise for Patricia Donat's
Chalk Dust, Red Tape and Miracles

"*Chalk Dust, Red Tape and Miracles* is a book written by and for dedicated teachers who are still committed to those idealistic notions that one small human being can change the world. This is a must-read for anyone thinking about elementary school teaching. It would also be a helpful addition to any school administrator's library and to parents who take an extra interest in the school environment. It is a gem of a book."

— Linda Stone Fish, Ph.D.
Program Director and Associate Professor
College for Human Development
Syracuse University

"I enjoyed reading the portion of your manuscript. Your plan makes great sense. I completely agree with your statement that no one wants to acknowledge that the simplest methods are usually the best. Thank you for educating first-graders for thirty years; you have made a great contribution to our society!"

— Diane Ravitch
Brookings Institution
Washington, D.C.

"The road from initial teacher preparation to in-service training to real success in the classroom is often a rocky one. Donat's "*Chalk Dust, Red Tape and Miracles*" closes that gap and provides the beginner and veteran alike with the positive mental outlook and specific skills needed to meet the challenge of teaching in the year 2000 and beyond."

— Alan G. Shuttleworth
Superintendent/Principal
Colfax Elementary School District
Colfax, California

"Love it, love it, love it! Should be required reading for all those aspiring to a teaching career, AND, to all those IN the career who are burning out."

— Norma Smith
Retired Teacher

"This book is destined to become a text book for recruiting, educating and inspiring future educators."

— Shirley Fish
Retired Librarian
Joliet Township High Schools

"Impressive ideological collection, wonderfully written, reflecting a wealth of knowledge and experience. A teacher hasn't mastered teaching until they've taught first grade."

— Denise Stevens
Teacher
Toms River, N.J.

"Vivid, poignant and inspiring account about one of the most challenging careers anyone can choose. A must read for anyone who is contemplating teaching as a profession!"

— Shackay Angacian
Graduate Student, Education
C.W. Post

"It is a needed resource book for pre-service teachers, who must gain insight into the mechanics of teaching. An extremely thorough, factual, heartfelt, common sense approach! A detailed road map garnered from years of dedicated service! *Chalk Dust Red Tape and Miracles* exemplifies excellence in the teaching profession!"

— F. Ronald Wright
Teacher

"*Chalk Dust Red Tape and Miracles* is an insightful and comprehensive resource, written with knowledge, love and compassion. This work is an inspirational, pedagogical treasure and I highly recommend it!"

— Catherine Traversa
Former Teacher

"Everyone who reads *Chalk Dust Red Tape and Miracles* will come away knowing more about the privilege of teaching and the honor in becoming a generative force in the lives of students. Parents will rejoice in this book. It is as much a gift to them as it is to future teachers!"

— Evelyn Dvorak-Meyer
Former Teacher

"Having spent almost 30 years in teaching, I found the information, philosophy, ideas and content presented in Pat Donat's book, *Chalk Dust, Red Tape and Miracles* to be helpful, inspiring and useful to a beginning teacher as well as a veteran teacher."

— Alyce Perry
Retired Teacher
Whittier, California

"No other professional could have written your teaching and behavioral chapters any better. Great work."

— Elizabeth Jung
Publishing (Sales)
Hendersonville, N.C.

"Joy to read. Each page conveyed thoughts that every teacher knows."

— Saramary Goldstein
Reading Teacher

CHALK DUST, Red Tape and *Miracles*

Teaching with Heart, Humor and Hope!

In grateful recognition for the opportunity to serve as an educator in the H.H.H. School District #5, I wish all who read this work will come to realize a deeper sense of the awesome responsibilities charged to all who teach, guide and care for our youth! With deepest respect and gratitude for allowing me to have the most fulfilling career of a lifetime!

Sincerely,

Patricia Donat

CHALK DUST, Red Tape and *Miracles*

Teaching with Heart, Humor and Hope!

by

Patricia Donat

Tri-Star Publishing • New York

Chalk Dust, Red Tape and Miracles

Printed in the United States of America

For information address:
Tri-Star Publishing

Library of Congress Cataloging in Publication Data
ISBN: 0-9664351-0-9
LCCN: 97-65432

Cover design by Michael Lawrence with artistic consultation by Linda Lawrence

In Loving Memory
of
MAUREEN MECHANIC,
who in life and death is
and
was the true embodiment of,
"Courage Personified"

Table of Contents

Acknowledgements

Each of us is born into this world and learns to rely on key people who by their talents, their dedication and their love, give to us special gifts that alter and enhance our lives in unique and meaningful ways. These wondrous individuals often are not aware of their importance. It is with deepest admiration and devotion that I hereby recognize the following people for changing my life at crucial times in significant ways. For without their guidance, this work may never have come to fruition!

To Sister Mary Florenz: 2nd Grade Teacher
Thank you for allowing a fledgling seven year old a chance to feel good about school. You were warm and non-threatening at a crucial time.

To Sister Mary Liam: 8th Grade Teacher
Thank you for allowing me to finish my elementary school experience on a high note. You applauded my individuality and gave me the confidence to go on to bigger and better things.

To Miss Beth Newlon: 11th Grade English Teacher
Thank you for opening up the world of language for me. I learned to love words and reading from you.

To Coleman Lyons: Superintendent of Schools
Thank you for giving me the chance to take the first and greatest professional step of my life. I will be forever grateful.

To Ellen Schoenberg: Interim 2nd Grade Teacher
Thank you for being such a warm and loving mentor. You showed me the creative way to teach.

To Dell Trayer: Colleague for 18 years
Thank you for putting up with all my plans and schemes. You were always my number one cohort and fan. You gave me the freedom to be me.

To Joseph R. Charette: Principal
Thank you for elevating me to many positions that allowed me to grow and change. Your confidence and leadership were invaluable.

To Debbie & Ed Blair: Principals
Thank you for your praise and your acceptance of my individuality. You allowed me the freedom to create.

To My Many Colleagues:
Thank you for the freedom to be myself as well as be a team player. Each of you taught me something of value.

To All My Students:

Thank you for being the real teachers.
You taught me how to teach and
how to learn. Each of you
touched my life in a very
special way and I will
never forget you.

To Kristen Slang: 1st Grade Teacher

Thank you for crossing my path and
giving me the opportunity to learn
mentoring. Your presence created
a reason to start this project.
This work is lovingly
dedicated to you and all
teachers!

To Kenna Flicker: Super Student Teacher

Thank you for renewing my faith in
the next generation of teachers to
come. Your maturity, dedication
and love proved to be the
impetus I needed to continue
this project!

To Linda Lawrence: Parent & family friend

Thank you for your faithful support
and the idea for this project. Your
encouragement and your artistry
has added so much to this
work. I'm truly grateful!

To John Donat: Brother and friend

Thank you for being born. You gave
me the impetus to choose the lifelong career that I love more
each year. You were my
special teacher!

To John Donat Sr. : Devoted Father

Thank you for your expertise with
words and reading. Your daily
example set the stage for this
work. I wish you could be
here to see it!

To Doris Donat: Devoted Mother

Thank you for the time, energy,
devotion and sacrifices you gave on
my behalf. Though your vision for
me was other than teaching,
your love and undying
support made all things
possible!
You taught me everything I know and
gave me the tools to grow into a
productive adult. I will forever
be in awe of the person you
are and the gift your life
has given me!

Joyfully,
Patricia Donat

Special Thanks

Marva Collins — Westside Preparatory School
Your enlightened philosophy makes you a true giant in our field and a mentor to all who wish to be called "teacher"!

Rabbi Marc Gellman — Noted & Honored Clergyman, Author, T. V. personality!
Your infinite wisdom, guidance, praise & support throughout my career are indelible gifts. You are a towering figure to and for all people to emulate!

Jack & Michael Lawrence — Family Friends
Your endless advice and computer support has been invaluable to this project!

Introduction

There is a deep human need within all of us, I believe, to leave a piece of ourselves behind when our earthly life is over. For many of us, this need is satisfied through the birth and raising of children, thus assuring our legacy. Others write great pieces of literature, perform fabulous physical feats, paint magnificent pictures, compose wondrous music, construct intricate buildings, statues or even cities. Still others become significant for the degree of humanity they bring to the world, whether as peacemakers, social workers or any of the myriad of helping professions.

We are also privileged to know of the many trailblazers who climb mountains, discover vaccines, or offer their lives to safeguard ours.

Each of us in whatever capacity longs for some kind of greatness. We want to leave the world a better place by our sheer presence. For many of us, our career is our life's work. We spend so many of our waking hours honing and refining our skills, teaching them to others and reaping the emotional rewards of our labors.

This humble work has taken one year to compile and complete, but it represents over thirty years of study, observation, and everyday experience in a first grade classroom. Over the years it has become apparent to me that in most cases, my own included, teacher training programs have fallen short of their intended mark. Prospective teachers are often found to be severely lacking in the background knowledge of the core liberal arts courses that form the foundation for teaching children in the curriculum areas. Also, in an attempt to teach educational theory by studying what is written, we have all been cheated out of the practical or daily happenings that can spell the difference between success and failure.

Knowing theory does not help when a child is not mastering a skill, or when a youngster acts out continually. Theories always sound good on paper, but often fall short in reality. One needs survival tools and a large degree of common sense. Spending six months to a year in practice teaching is not sufficient.

It is also apparent to me that many young people are choosing the teaching field for the wrong reasons. They don't have the slightest clue as to the enormity of the task teachers undertake. Therefore, this work attempts to explain, detail, delight in and at times glorify the art and the practicality of teaching as a career.

I've tried to discuss and bring to light real situations that have occurred in the classroom of a first year teacher. The trials, fears, frustrations, successes, problems, questions and situations have been chronicled here to become a guide to others. It is also hoped that an accurate picture of teaching has been depicted. I've attempted to instruct and give support to a new recruit in the hopes that the many pressures felt by all of us do not dampen her motivation and her desire to continually learn and eventually become a great educator.

Also, I have used this work as a forum to present my philosophy, not only in theory, but certainly in practice. I want to spell out my dreams for an ideal school situation and give some idea of the deep concerns that

I have for the future of education in the twenty-first century. In some cases we have lost valuable subjects and skills that I feel are crucial to obtaining a real education. Then too, my position on parenting skills and their relationship to the educational progress we either cooperatively achieve, or fail to make, is a recurring theme running through this work.

Next, I'd like to bring a chuckle to the many members of our profession who have left the ranks to go on to other endeavors. I hope this description of school in general rings true to them and puts these veterans in a nostalgic frame of mind. I'd like the educators of the past to know that some things still exist for better or worse, the way they always did. Also, I'd like them to know that in small pockets of the country, education IS alive and well, but that there is definitely real reason for concern.

Lastly, I hope that the readers of this work come to know and love teaching the way I do. I would like everyone to develop a healthy respect for first graders and those lucky individuals who teach them. Six year olds have an enormous job to do in learning how to read and become serious students. They are often maligned and thought less of when in reality they are on the brink of something BIG, namely the beginning of the formal part of their education. They need master teachers to awaken in them a real desire to overcome early fears and to develop competent skills in order to become life-long learners and productive, fulfilled citizens. It is to this end, that I have lovingly and purposefully put "pen to paper" !

Sincerely,
Patricia Donat

CHALK DUST, Red Tape and Miracles

Teaching with Heart, Humor and Hope!

Chapter 1

August 30th

Dear Kristen,

Welcome to our school family and in particular, congratulations on obtaining your first teaching job in first grade! It is quite an honor to be selected to begin your career in the most crucial grade of all.

This will be a tough year for you, but an important learning year. Keep your eyes and ears open to everything in your environment. Try to make your classroom a place of respect, stimulation , understanding and LOVE ! You will hear the opinions of many for advice is easy to give. Filter everything you hear and see through your own mind and heart and do what is right for YOU!

As for the parents, always try to be fair and put yourself in their shoes. For better or worse, this is their beloved youngster, flesh of their flesh. It's not easy to hear bad news about the child one has created. Always say something positive even when that is not the focus of the call or note in question. Keeping hope alive makes it easier for a parent to have confidence in you and to work cooperatively for the benefit of the youngster. It's crucial to win the respect, admiration and love of the parents in your room. Without their support you operate in a vacuum and you may only achieve minimum goals. Besides children need to see their parents in school, actively involved in their child's education. It is this motivational praise that helps you change or modify behavior and make academic advances as well.

Always remember to be yourself; anything less will thwart your efforts and lessen your impact. Children can spot a phony and they will never have the respect necessary to aid in their emotional and academic growth. It's not a crime to be a beginner. We all have to start somewhere. Your youth will add a freshness to the staff and an energy to your program. What you lack in experience you can compensate for in intelligence , motivation and just plain old fashioned common sense and HARD work.

Think about your own personal goals for the year, as well as what you want your students to take from this year. You will always remember your first class with a special deep feeling. Don't try to be their friend! You are their teacher and that is an awesome responsibility. Teaching is only surpassed by Motherhood in importance as careers go. Being an educator is not a job but a calling of the highest order. For you have the power within your hands to either make or break a child. As a role model, you are always on display. Every word, every look, your body language, what and how you speak and even what you DON'T say are all subject to constant scrutiny by everyone around you. Just try to teach the way you have always dreamed your ideal experience to have been as a young child. Try to be consistent and fair at all times. Talk to your class about things important to you and to them. You'll find that they are very bright and knowledgeable and generally accurate within their range of experience. Enjoy them! Don't be afraid to laugh at a situation. Get "under their skins" by allowing them to know you and feel comfortable in your presence. Create a family atmosphere, binding them together right from the start. Establish rules and offer support at all times to gain their respect and admiration. Love them! A smile, a pat on the back, a hand shake, a deserved compliment goes a long, long way. The children of today are sorely lacking in real attention. They are showered with material wealth and experiences for the most part, but they tend to value little. Be an old-fashioned young teacher. Give them the basics and limit the fringes. They will face a world where competition is vastly increased and diversity is crucial. They must be able to think, make decisions and be adaptable. Be clear and concise with your directions. Think of many different ways to explain the same thing. Repeat, repeat and repeat again. Don't underestimate the power of drill. It's old-fashioned, but it works. Always remember that they are only six years old. Tell them they are wonderful every day in a thousand ways collectively and singly. Learning to read is an awesome task for them. It requires breaking a code that they are unaware of. To do this they MUST take a risk and that is so hard for some. The quiet child will try to escape you. Find out why.

Remember that each day is a new beginning, another chance for you to reach that shy child or the acting out one or the "motor mouth" or the unmotivated one. The energy that you will need to achieve your goals is enormous, but the fulfillment is unparalleled! In expressing yourself, you are shaping tomorrow for each child placed in your care. The task never gets easier. It always becomes more challenging!

Congratulations to you, Kristen and good luck! You have entered into a very privileged group of people. YOU ARE A TEACHER !!!!!

Fondly,
Patricia Donat

Chapter 2

September 25th

Dear Kristen,

Congratulations! You made it over the first major hurdle of your career. Hopefully, this will be the first of many Open School Nights you will experience. To many educators this evening is feared beyond belief. Meeting and speaking eloquently and with authority is crucial to gaining confidence right at the start.

There is no substitute for adequate planning, organization and mental preparation for such an event. You demonstrated the ability to handle all three and therefore your success was assured. Also, I know that you were able to communicate your philosophy in the language of the heart. That is something one cannot disguise. It comes across all over your face. One either cares deeply or one takes the shallow road.

I'm glad this experience went well for you. You've now passed through the starting gate. However, the race is just beginning. Now it is your task to deliver on the promises you have made. Much like a political candidate, you must keep your constituents happy. This is an awesome task that you have undertaken.

Each child must be challenged to perform at his or her personal best in all subject areas. Furthermore, and most important, each child must develop the work habits, self-motivation and the desire to learn. They must see the value in the skills taught, feel growth in their own self worth and certainly they must be rewarded for their daily efforts with huge doses of loving discipline. When a child feels that a teacher works hard, appreciates and loves them, one can over time make tremendous progress.

Children must learn to work cooperatively, with joy and zest. They must feel the need to know and then they will take the risks necessary to learn. Six year olds are like sponges. They begin by wanting to please. They look for facial expressions and praise. As they feel successful, children generally become more confident and independent. As a teacher, you are their cheerleader and staunch supporter. They count on you for fairness, justice, knowledge, understanding, forgiveness and love. It's a "tall order", something that good teachers strive for year after year.

Remember that each child comes to the learning situation with varying strengths and weakness. They come from different backgrounds and they exhibit varying degrees of desire and maturity. Parents also have definite expectations which can exert a marked influence on a child's progress or lack of it. A typical class contains children of varying ages as well. An entire year can separate the oldest from the youngest. This factor alone can play an enormous role in the scheme of things. Physical traits cannot be overlooked in dealing with children, for this category also accounts for tremendous differences. Even birth order must be looked at when planning and predicting appropriate expectations for children.

To be sure, parents play a powerful part in executing your academic plans. They expect your best at all times, and gaining their confidence requires hard work and energy plus flawless timing. Parents are notorious for comparing notes and talking in front of their children. They see you as an employee, but also as a substitute parent. They can be demanding, but at times they are intimidated by some of the things we say. It's a delicate balance that one must achieve. We need the parents to support and respect us. It's a constant give and take and as teachers we must continually orchestrate and refine the relationships we initiate each year. To do anything less is unthinkable. Parents are often as fragile as the children they send us each day. They alternate between the need to be educated and the desire to be coddled. They unknowingly communicate their own fears, anxieties and weakness to their children. To be sure, some are extremely lacking in parenting skills and therefore, they look to you for guidance. Always remember that each child is a product of his or her environment. Acceptable behavior can vary enormously from family to family. Also, the incidence of step-families and single parent homes has increased dramatically over the years. This can change the whole complexion of a classroom of students. Then to, we find ourselves in an age where in many cases, both parents are working. Unfortunately, this means parents have to struggle to spend quality time with their youngsters. Even in cases where mothers are home, children are often over-programmed with after school activities and play dates. Family time is often relegated to weekends at best.

It often seems that education is given a rear seat, even in the homes of well meaning parents. Socialization and peer group experiences are the order of the day. Parents seem obsessed with providing exposure to sports, dance, musical instruments and the like, sometimes way before a child is physically, mentally or socially able to succeed at the skills necessary to enjoy these activities. This can create a situation where a child is programmed for failure. Often this translates to schoolwork as well.

Also, the parents of today seem to want to provide more material benefits than children actually request or require. They have confused the need for wealth with the need for spending quality time with children. Sleep-away camp has replaced the family vacation. Computer and video games have replaced an evening of board games, reading and round table discussions. The old-fashioned birthday at home with ten neighborhood friends has been replaced by bowling, amusement or craft parties at local stores set up for that purpose. Upwards of twenty children are usually assembled for such celebrations. Fun is now measured by bigger, better, louder and definitely more expensive. Such "shows" make our job much more difficult.

It will also become obvious to you over time that children are by and large more verbal than we were. This could be due to the fact that young children are often privy to adult conversations that they can not possibly understand. They will use words incorrectly, but be unable to use language commensurate with their age. Also, the children of today are allowed to make choices that often seem inappropriate for their age. For example, a six year old might be asked, "What would you like for dinner? " or " Do you want to wear your jacket today? " These practices translate into developing a child who directs and demands on a regular basis. Thus when asked to pick up a crayon from the floor, a typical child might reply, "It's not mine!"

So, given all of the above influences, values and backgrounds, not to mention the individuality of each child, it's an awesome job to juggle all of this mentally while trying to teach effective lessons.

Also, children seem to be less and less able to listen carefully. They are spoiled with the excitement and drama as seen daily on television and in the movies. They somehow expect teachers to duplicate these entertainment forms in the classroom. When this doesn't happen, they often become disillusioned with school. The many hours of programmed viewing has made some children less able to communicate effectively, to relate cooperatively to peers and adults and often we even find children who are somewhat resistant to human contact. They seem to prefer the passivity of taking in stimuli for purely entertainment purposes. Therefore, it becomes easy for some children to tune us in or out, just as they do with the computer, the video game or the television. We teach, but they often listen selectively. So in effect the media becomes our competition.

To be sure, we as teachers are ultimately challenged to be the "master of ceremonies" in our classrooms. It is there that we need to muster all the enthusiasm, knowledge and love that we have within us. We must do this every day, when we are happy, when we are depressed, when we feel great and even when we are "under the weather". The future of our country and our world depends on the efforts each of us put forth. Our children deserve the best education we can afford to give them. Anything less amounts to cheating them out of their rightful inheritance. Becoming literate is not a luxury, but a necessity. Our future realistically depends on the generation that follows us. They will ultimately run our government, defend our borders and change the face of the world in many ways. Our influence individually and collectively cannot be underestimated!

Your career is just beginning, Kristen! Look at the wonder you see on those bright faces each day. Lose yourself in their lives, their needs and their successes. The rewards will be many, but they will be of the intangible kind. Always remember, the child you save with your love may be the child who grows up to become a leader, a doer, a saver! You are the cheerleader, the ringmaster, the conductor! Give it your all!

Fondly,
Pat

Chapter 3

October 6th

Dear Kristen,

So you have "Zachary"! You're going to be challenged right at the start of your career. That's a blessing in disguise, although you may not appreciate that now. You might as well know from the beginning that there will probably be at least one "Zachary" every year. He'll come in different sizes and appearances, but "Zachary" will be there full of energy, ready to challenge every day you'll spend with him. Make the most of your experience with "Zachary". He will test your powers of concentration and your desire to teach. He'll push you to the limit and force your patient nature. On the other hand, "Zachary" will teach you more about child development and parenting than any book ever written. His demanding personality could touch you deeply and show you in a very special way what love is really all about. This, "Zachary" will do for you, if you let him!

Educators on every level have always been saddled with the threat of children with "behavior" problems. They can destroy the character of a whole class if allowed to do so. Like an infectious disease, a negative child can erode the academic framework that exists in a classroom, thereby altering significantly in some cases the progress made by each child.

Unfortunately, some teachers become disillusioned with the "Zacharys" of our world. Such children are usually so demanding that teachers give up under the guise that it's unfair to spend an inordinate amount of time with just one child. It's easy to understand how a teacher could feel that way. On the surface, it's a correct assumption. However, we are not dealing with an easy issue here. It's not a question of apples vs. oranges . We are in effect passing judgment on a child's life. Well, what are the alternatives? Often such children end up in special education programs or even special schools, where they are placed with children who have similar problems. More often than not they will only learn to model behavior that is worse than that which they already exhibit.

To really take on a "Zachary" requires a high degree of dedication, not to mention the energy and patience of a saint. Why do it, you say? Simply put, you might be "Zachary's" only chance at normalcy and a real life. If you question everyone who knows "Zachary", you'll probably find some or all of the reasons why he is exhibiting acting out behaviors. He could be an only child, who has limited access to peers and therefore is not at all adept in social skills. Loneliness can cause a child to seek the negative in a desperate attempt to get attention. Perhaps he is a child of working parents, who is forced to spend afternoons in front of a television or with an aging grandparent. Maybe "Zachary" is a child of divorced parents, who is shuttled back and forth between bickering adults, obsessed with the fight over him. He could even be the youngest in a home where the siblings are teens or even college age. Whatever it is spend time finding out as much as you can about "Zachary's" background. It's a first step in educating yourself about this troubled child. Remember, children with discipline problems aren't born, they are a product of their environment.

Knowing where a child comes from also includes delving into his physical health and his academic strengths and weaknesses. Check for accurate abilities to see and hear as well as to process information. A child who is not learning is sure to become a discipline problem. If he is not achieving for some physical reason, then that must be addressed. The frustration felt by some children can be overwhelming. They don't realize that something is wrong with them. They feel inept and unsuccessful. Often they become social outcasts. They lose the desire to learn, because it is too hard. When fulfillment is lacking in a child's life, it becomes visible in their behavior. It's a vicious cycle, one that must be broken by a caring and dedicated teacher!

So here you are, juggling your time, energy and talents among twenty-one children. You work hard, plan your lessons effectively and still "Zachary" keeps the pressure on by daily testing rules, decisions and routines. He seems to need constant reminders about his behavior and though you feel you give him enough attention, he always seems to require or demand more. At the end of the day you are drained from the strain of teaching, observing , evaluating and just plain living with "Zachary" in a room full of other youngsters.

Often you feel you are losing the battle. "Zachary" is tormenting his peers and making it difficult for you to teach. Worst of all, other children may be picking up his negativism and could begin to model his behavior. What can you do?

There is no easy answer! And there is no sure cure for what ails "Zachary". His only hope is to be taught by a loving teacher. You see, "Zachary" is screaming for attention. He selfishly sees himself as the only one in the class when that is to his advantage. At other times he enjoys being the "class clown" or the aggressor. In any case, to ignore him will only further annoy and frustrate him. Yelling or admonishing "Zachary" in a loud voice will only assure him that you are the enemy. Your negative reaction will only fuel his antisocial behavior. Isolating him from the other children may be a short term solution, but over time he will learn that he is unloved and unworthy of attention, even of the negative kind.

Over the years, I've been fortunate to know many "Zacharys". I find that generally it is best to have this special child in as close proximity to the teacher as possible. I'd put my arm around him while he is attempting to read. I'd hover over him while he writes. I'd pat his hand at the smallest success or improvement. I'd speak firmly but lovingly with and to him, making sure that I have close and complete eye contact. This assures me that he is tuned in to what I am saying. I'd repeat directions often in clear and simple speech. I'd encourage modeling appropriate behaviors exhibited by others. I'd watch him continuously, never letting him go anywhere alone or move about the room without a significant reason. I'd praise his efforts to obey my instructions and I'd forgive gently when I feel that he really tried. When "Zachary" masters the smallest step, I'd point it out to him so that he feels the success. I'd applaud his efforts and have the class do so as well. I'd accept setbacks as inevitable and put him on the bus with a smile, remembering that tomorrow is another day.

Now, you may get the feeling that this is an all encompassing job. Well you're right and for a time it may seem to you that the other children are being cheated. I don't think so, though it took me awhile to feel this way. You see, the class is learning a valuable lesson while "Zachary" is being deprogrammed. They are learning the art of handling a different child. They will grow in respect and admiration for you and more importantly they will change their view of "Zachary" as a trouble-maker, because you consider him worth your time and effort. That alone could, over time help to significantly alter "Zachary's" behavior.

Above all, I'd meet "Zachary" at the door each day and not let him step inside until I warmly encouraged him to start the day right, reviewing just what he is expected to do. I'd tell him often that he is a smart and a handsome boy and as such, he does not need to engage in problematic behavior. I'd work on his social skills by setting up visits to his home by appropriate classmates if possible. I'd seat him near children I want him to emulate. When he is able to work independently for short periods of time, I'd be sure to recognize his efforts. I'd have him come early or stay after for extra help. The extra attention, plus the growth in skill areas will surely increase his feelings of self worth and give him the confidence to keep improving.

In short, you have to allow "Zachary" to get under your skin and that way, YOU will be able to make a dent in his fragile personality. You see, he probably trusts no one. That is a sad state of affairs, because until he learns to believe in you, he will not learn anything academic and he will not be able to alter his behavior enough to fit in with accepted standards. "Zachary" is on a collision course. He already has a reputation as being disruptive. In order to break the cycle of negativism and punishment, he must learn that there are greater rewards for acceptable behavior. These are outward signs of acceptance and warmth, cheers from peers and over time the deep feelings of self worth that propel us all to do more and be more.

Admittedly, all of the above may NOT work! There are always cases of children who are so severely disturbed that they must be removed from the regular class situation. This, however is an extreme measure which is the result of a group decision and exhaustive testing. There are many alternative forms of instruction for such children, but I would definitely give "Zachary" the benefit of time. First grade is a hard adjustment for most children and for a difficult child who has not tasted success, it must be frightening.

"Zachary" needs time to grow and find himself in an environment where he feels structure, discipline and love. He needs to know there are limits and privileges and that he will be treated as fairly as everyone else. He must grow into his body and soul, realizing that his physical strength is something that must not be mishandled. "Zachary" must come to trust the adults around him and learn to take the risks necessary to learn. As he amasses academic and social skills, he will gain the confidence necessary to become more independent. These steps will allow him to feel good about himself as a person and to take joy in his accomplishments. All this we can do for "Zachary", if we give him the time and energy he needs.

So you have "Zachary"! Little do you know it, but you'll never forget him. You might even grow to love him in that special way that teachers often do. With any luck "Zachary" will grow up to be someone special and maybe even someone important in our world. Many famous people started their lives in worse shape than "Zachary" and many of them pulled themselves out of the mire.

Don't ever underestimate the power you can exert over the "Zachary's" of the world. I'm counting on you, Kristen and so is "Zachary"!

Fondly,
Pat

Chapter 4

October 19th

Dear Kristen,

I guess the "honeymoon" is over! It was bound to happen you know. Now you are in for a permanent dose of reality. We've headed full force into the first marking period. Fall is definitely here, just as sure as the children stop wearing shorts and the flood of paperwork resembles the rapidly falling leaves outside your window.

Everything seems to hit you all at once. The heat and the lethargy of September has faded and the crisp cool air has heralded a return to overcrowded schedules, multiple meetings, incessant phone calls, endless planning, working lunches and sixteen hour days.

Suddenly, every department that had the luxury of testing and arranging schedules and classes during September has now descended upon us with the results of their labors. Proudly, they come to us with our carefully plotted time slot. By the time we digest the fact that reading, speech, resource, E.S.L., computers, health and occupational therapy have now been added to our weekly cadre of educational experiences, we begin to realize that we really need to be skilled jugglers to handle all of the above. As we sink into a sitting position at the end of the day, we can honestly say that there is no mention of this kind of confusion in the "how to" book. In fact, there is NO "how to" book to speak of at all!

So, we summon all the creativity and determination we can muster to attack the nightmare of making a complicated schedule come alive. It all looks so possible on paper. Ha! Just try getting twenty first graders to Music class in the B wing of the building by 9:15 when they have winter coats, boots, backpacks etc. to dispose of, not to mention notes, complaints, bus problems and fights in the hall to unload on us. All the experience in the world does not make some things easier. You just learn to somehow take it all in stride.

Then, after a week of said schedule, you begin to see a pattern emerging. First, it is a rarity to have the pleasure of teaching or even seeing your whole class all together. Worse than that, you realize that the same children are inevitably being pulled out all the time, thus totally fragmenting their day. These are the very children who desperately need the security and stability of one teacher and a predictable routine. Believe me, I hear your frustration. Our task is now that much more difficult but we, the classroom teachers are still ultimately charged with educating all the children placed under our care!

How does one do that, when there are a host of other non-incidentals to occupy our time? No one ever mentioned the flood of secretarial responsibilities foisted on teachers. In September we are given the B.E.D.S. form, courtesy of the state. I wonder if the educational data compiled throughout the four corners will contribute in any way to the betterment of teaching and ultimately, learning in our schools. The office cranks out numerous memos, letters, forms, deadlines, edicts, requests, lists and the like, all requiring scads of paper that magically end up in our mailboxes. Sometimes I feel like my mailbox may come down with a terminal case of claustrophobia caused by "paperitis"! Needless to say, all of the above documents require immediate personal attention and were due yesterday!

Worse than the above, however is the inevitable reawakening of the infamous P.T.A. This prestigious organization is more a P.A. than a P.T.A. They spend the summers lounging and then by Fall they are raring to go!

Under the guise of fund raising, these homemakers are really into sleuthing. They become involved in all sorts of committees that have nothing whatever to do with education. In effect, the P.T.A. has single-handedly turned our schools into a major business concern. These ladies are in charge of the Wrapping Paper Committee, the Book Fairs, the Fashion Show, the Holiday Sale, the Carnival, the Fifth Grade Graduation party, the Teacher Recognition Day Luncheon, the Opening Day Luncheon, the After School Program etc., etc., etc.! Most of these functions require forms, many notices, and payments that must be returned to school and funneled through our hands. The time wasted by us in folding, separating, categorizing, enveloping and distributing said returns is enormous. The beginning of every day is taken up with secretarial chores, including compiling absence notes, issuing bus passes, taking attendance, reading parent requests and handling P.T.A. business. It all gets to be overwhelming, especially for the starry-eyed novice with high ideals or the veteran who desperately wants to return to the days when teachers were actually free to teach! The on the job training in paperwork that one gets as a teacher could definitely prepare you to be the C.E.O. of any major corporation! The only difference is that in big business one has a staff to handle these trivialities. In stark contrast, teachers are a one-man show handling a three ring circus!

Admittedly, all this is enough to cope with on a daily basis, but we also have to suffer through Open Education Week, a celebration that encourages parents to see their schools in action. Now, the idea of making classrooms open and accessible is an admirable one. However, it's unfeasible to think that twenty sets of parents can view any kind of education going on in a room that with furniture etc. can barely hold twenty children and one harried teacher. Naturally, we must also mention the excitement felt by children in such a circumstance. It can only be termed stressful and probably not realistic. How often are we invited to see Lilco or A.T.T. or the post office in operation. We can barely decipher their bills and they don't really care what we think about their service.

Children are a special kind of commodity. It seems that everyone always has their best interests at heart. Parents feel and rightly so that they pay high taxes and should be afforded every opportunity to see what their money buys. I've always felt that this need could be met by the installation of one-way mirrors in classrooms. This would allow everyone access to a natural setting at any time. The by-product of such an arrangement might even be the elevation of teaching and learning to more acceptable levels. However, I doubt that many educators would agree with me on this one! So much for the perils of Open School Week.

Of course, you realize that you must be observed formally four times per year as long as you remain untenured. These are also stressful situations, because you feel so much is at stake and it is. However, I have always used these opportunities to try teaching a tough skill in a new and more creative way. I've always grown through these experiences and have felt a surge of accomplishment after I recovered from the strain. It seems like these forty-five minute visits are really lasting all day. Usually, the children are most cooperative, because they view these principal visits as a chance to "show off" and first graders are notorious for looking for any opportunity to "show their wares"!

Try to relax and be yourself. Do something that is comfortable for you. I always suggest starting with math and planning your lesson for the morning when the children are wide awake. Math is exciting, because it is active and there are so many relationships that one can cull from most lessons. Keep the children focused and on their toes. Walk around as you talk and redirect children who are wandering. Praise the efforts of individual children as much as possible, for that is how you insure continued success. Ask thought provoking questions on many levels, so that you can probe into the depth of each child's thought process. Wait during questioning, as children tend to "freeze" when put on the spot. Adults do too! The extra time gives the nervous child a chance to recoup and possibly come up a winner. It also tells children that you realize that they are doing their best to please you. Waiting reinforces a confidence in you as someone who understands differences. Always explain the purpose of the visit and your expectations. That tends to ensure cooperation and team spirit, both of which you need to be successful. By getting the children on your side and making them become an integral and important part of the visit, you cement your relationship with them and incur their valuable support! Don't worry. Once you start, you become so focused that the whole experience will fly by in record time. You can do it, I know!

Just think! In a few hours you can once again face the dreaded dismissal muddle. As you've already noticed, the time between 2:45 and 3:15 seems to be thought of by parents as the "erroneous zone". It's the end of the day and the time that all "hell breaks loose".

We as teachers are at a definite disadvantage, because we often are not aware of the other agenda that occurs like clockwork right at the end of the day. It's almost as if everyone "changes hats" and begins the next part of their day. The office goes into full swing and the calling begins. There will be days when it seems like every child in the building is being dismissed early. Wait until it snows!!! You will see a mass departure that will rival the supposed end of the world!

There is the case of James who needs to meet his tennis group and Suzie who is going to dance class. Sarah has a horse-back riding lesson and Jeffrey needs a haircut. Mark has a skating lesson and Scott, Tara and Michelle go to religion class. Then we have the infamous after school activities program. Peter, Amy and Jamie are attending cooking class. Jon and David have karate class, while Megan and Laurie stay for arts and crafts. Now mind you, there are always a few children who are riding on different buses because they have pre-arranged play dates.

You've probably figured out by now that upwards of half your class has magically disappeared right before your eyes. They've gone off to "greener pastures" to spend some FREE TIME. Each day is different you know. I sometimes have nightmares about losing my many lists. During stormy days, I truly wish that my mother would call for my early dismissal!

Well, if you manage to send or dismiss everyone going to the right places, you might be able to lead the leftover "deprived" youngsters to their respective buses. However, that is not so simple. As you make your way through the hallowed halls, you become enmeshed in a traffic jam of monumental proportions. Classes are assembling from two directions heading for the one intersection through which everyone must pass. As you approach the office, you see hordes of parents still waiting for their dismissed cherubs. They mill around exchanging pleasantries, carrying babies and inching their way closer and closer, blocking the exit door in a full scale manner. If you manage to get through this bottle-neck, you are truly eligible for an award, but don't expect any accolades. You'll surely have to repeat this chore on a daily basis.

Once outside you notice that the buses are never in the same order. In the rain they are barely even visible. As you call the bus numbers and watch each child ascend the steps of their respective buses, you hope that you make it to the end of the line without incident. Inevitably, you'll find that you have one child left over. As he or she starts to cry, you summon the last ounce of strength within you not to lose your cool. You take comfort in the fact that there are other classes behind you and with any luck you can retrace your steps and find the correct bus before the said youngster dissolves into a puddle of tears. With any luck you accomplish this feat before 3:30. Take refuge, in a few weeks you'll have the privilege of being on Bus Duty.

This wonderful week long task is one that teachers consider a major annoyance. You won't be alone, however. Two other lucky individuals will share the responsibility with you. It's really not so bad; it just requires the sight of an eagle, the skills of a traffic cop and the endurance of a weatherman doing field work. Try watching seven hundred children literally zooming off their respective buses and bolting head-long for two sets of open doors. It closely resembles watching horses coming out of the starting gate at Churchill Downs. At the end of the day, each of the three teachers is strategically placed and ready to view the endless line of classes in somewhat imperfect order. In wind, rain, snow, hail, or storm, the Bus Duty teachers are at their posts, as loyal as the predictable mailman. They keep everyone moving, watch for late buses, check off classes on their rain-soaked lists and are ever mindful of a stray child or an unwanted adult. It all sounds so foreign, I'm sure. Fear not, you'll have at least three more chances to practice your new responsibility later in the year!

Perhaps you are beginning to see how many tasks teachers handle each day that have nothing whatever to do with teaching. Some of them are strictly public relations activities, like Open School Week. Others are purely inconsequential paperwork that complicates our lives and robs of us of precious teaching time. Still other responsibilities are in place to safeguard children, like Bus Duty. In any case we are bound by these frustrations until something else comes along to replace them, knowing that nothing will really change for the better.

Always remember what we are all really here for. Never lose your prospective amid the paperwork, the headaches, the long hours and the endless interruptions. Your children need to stay focused on the task at hand. Maybe we are also charged to serve as buffers between endless red tape and a child's education. It's a tall order, surviving each day. You don't get combat pay, but a smile, a warm hello or an occasional note somehow makes up for it all! Don't knuckle under! Someday, YOU'LL be a veteran!

Warmly,
Pat

Chapter 5

October 26th

Dear Kristen,

You've undoubtedly noticed the slight chill in the air lately. The leaves have magically become transformed into their magnificent fall colors and pumpkins are definitely in abundance.

This is always the time of year when everything and everyone starts to operate in high gear. We begin to zoom rather rapidly from one activity into another with scarcely any time to breathe. Perhaps the crisp air energizes everyone and reminds us that there is so little active time before the cold, quiet of winter makes its presence known and felt.

One of the highlights of the fall season is the P.T.A. sponsored Fashion Show. It is a gala evening to be sure, a chance for all the mothers to strut their fancy duds and act important. You can't imagine the enormity of this event. It closely resembles a wedding in every way. The tables are artistically decorated and there are what seems like millions of prizes, ranging anywhere from a coupon for a flying saucer at Carvel to a weekend in New York City.

It always amazes me to see the unbelievable transformation that occurs that evening. The mothers who saunter in at 3:15 in tennis skirts and warm-up suits suddenly appear in sequins, mini skirts and see-through dresses. It's so comical to watch the hidden competition and the overt attempts to be friendly and down-right inquisitive at what's billed as a purely social evening. Most of the time I've felt I was "on stage" as much as the models were.

Usually the evening drags on quite late due to all the raffles that are awarded. The committee truly works hard to plan and execute such an event. They visibly wallow in the accolades of the audience and I often wonder how much of a "high" one can get in such a situation. I often think of the profits of the event and I wish that we had some real input into how the money is spent. Well, I'm sure you'll find the experience interesting to say the least.

Of course you know that Halloween is just around the corner. This has to be an all time favorite with first graders. They start talking about Halloween the minute October rolls around. This holiday seems to bring out the fantasies that six year olds really enjoy. Boys revel in donning the Ninja, Batman, and action figure character costumes. Girls still enjoy dressing up as the tried and true Cinderella, fairy godmother, bride or even Scarlet O'Hara. The anticipation of the event builds as the end of the month draws near. It's great fun to try to guess what everyone is planning to wear on that day. Some little people just cannot contain themselves for the month and must divulge the nature of their costume. I for one enjoy watching their excitement and reveling in one of the last strongholds of childhood.

When Halloween arrives you can sense the furor of activity building. All sorts of projects and party planning has preceded the momentous day. Children bound in the door as if they are heading for the Disney World gate, costumes and make-up bagged, waiting for the fun to begin. Parents begin arriving by 1:30 for the 2:00 parade. Many need to help dress their little darlings. This includes sophisticated make-up sessions that are quite professional in nature. Some of the parents dress up as well, which definitely adds to the fun. Pictures are taken everywhere as all the spectators line the parade route, which winds through the school and outside as well. Eerie music is blasted through the loud speaker to help put everyone in the mood. Naturally a large banner is carried by the costumed leaders. One year I remember being led by the "Fruit of the Loom" characters. It was quite imaginative to say the least. Needless to say, all classes attach themselves to this tribe of mixed characters and the whole atmosphere resembles what the Mardi Gras in New Orleans must be like. Everyone from toddlers to grandparents view the parade and it's a feeling of really being "on display". The myriad of costumes is a sight to see, showing creativity but sadly there is a definite attempt to outdo one's neighbor.

Once inside the party begins in earnest with treats, games and perhaps more pictures. Exhaustion starts to show and as the last child boards the bus, I'm always grateful that a safe and good time was had by all. Naturally, I begin thinking of an appropriate costume for next year while so many possibilities are fresh in my mind.

By November first, I realize that time is really flying. The children view the next calendar and think Hanukkah and Christmas are here, altogether forgetting the wonderful celebration of Thanksgiving. Somehow the historical nature of Thanksgiving is beyond first graders. They function better with concrete learnings. It's very difficult for them to understand and assimilate the knowledge necessary to fully appreciate this holiday. First of all, time concepts relating to other than the present are extremely difficult for young children to envision. This age group hasn't attained the maturity to be able to visualize an era that they have not experienced. Then to, the brutally hard lifestyle of the 1600's is completely out of character with today's standards. However, it is crucial to begin to orient children to the study of other cultures in order to broaden their base of reference and better able them to come to grips with the issues of life they will face in the year 2000 and beyond!

Many classes still celebrate a mock Thanksgiving by creating costumes, preparing a feast of sorts as well as reading, writing and studying all of the customs, events and the significance of this original American holiday!

Needless to say once December rolls around and the pace picks up to what can only be described as frenetic, the children have only one thing on their minds and that is creating a wish list for Hanukkah and/or Christmas. Naturally, you can expect hushed comparisons over which holiday is BETTER! Overwhelmingly, first graders assume that Hanukkah wins because you are awarded presents for eight straight days. It never occurs to them that despite the fact that Christmas is celebrated on one day, it is conceivable for many children to receive more than eight presents in one day! Well, so much for equality, concrete math and the childlike comparison of two holidays that are individually so beautifully packed with enduring significance!

I prefer to treat these holidays as separate entities even when they come together as sometimes is the case. More often than not Chanukah comes first. The miracle of the oil becomes more fascinating to me each year, as I am a staunch believer in such occurrences. Children need to learn that despite the awesome technology we are privileged to live with there still are the inexplicable happenings that keep alive the wonderment of childhood and life itself. Realizing that there is a power greater than we are at work in our world, whether it be scientific or religious in nature is a healthy thing. The advent of action figures, video games, movies and comic book heros has in many cases given children and even teens the inaccurate feeling that we are somehow invincible. Chanukah with its lights, foods, songs and games brings us back to a simpler time when being together as a family was more than enough for everyone. Its message of peace, joy and sharing however is diminished and blown completely out of proportion through merchandising and packaging begun in order to compete on a monetary level with Christmas. Sadly, we are all the worse off for it!

When Christmas finally comes, we are all on vacation. Perhaps that is another reason why Christmas loses face in the minds of first graders. It is impossible for them to report on the gifts they received when their peers are away! Because six year olds are very possessive as well as competitive, this vital experience is lost to them. Rarely do I hear of the family gatherings that occurred at Christmas or the holiday carols that were sung, the services attended or the kindnesses extended to the disadvantaged.

Attention is only given to the financial aspects of

the holiday. Thus the very beautiful birth of a special child who is believed to have been born into the world destined for greatness is a miracle that seemingly cannot compare with the likes of Disney or Steven Spielberg. The whole significance of this simple holiday once again fades into the pre-packaged version perpetrated on society by greedy retailers. Surely the children of the nineties must believe in their collective hearts that Chanukah and Christmas are holidays that come from a mall! Today the greatness of the simplistic must be made over into the spectacular and grandiose or it won't sell!

So as exhaustion overtakes everyone, we rejoice in a few days of relative respite. However, all too soon the New Year dawns with the sometimes gray, snowy and windy skies of winter, often stark and bleak in nature. During this time we reflect on the lives of Martin Luther King, Jr. as well as Presidents George Washington, and Abraham Lincoln and we continue with the Women's History movement in conjunction with our social studies curriculum. Children love to learn about real people, who through hard work became larger than life heros. This is an excellent opportunity to enlarge, embellish and otherwise inundate children with powerful vocabulary and valuable concepts, not to mention establishing a healthy respect for the part geography plays in all of our lives!

With the advent of spring and the appearance of a watery sun, colorful crocuses and the elusive Ground Hog, children have the golden opportunity to view the yearly change of seasons up close and personal. Although scientifically definable, the rebirth of that which withered and died the fall before still continues to evoke a sense of wonderment within me. Seemingly before our eyes all manner of blossoms appear, not to mention the abundance of vegetables and fruits as well as baby animals. Surprisingly six year olds who notice new outfits, a change of hair styles and can easily recall the names of those present at a birthday party, need enormous coaxing to be made aware of the subtle changes that slowly occur in weather patterns, familial activities and the wonders of the life cycle in our environment. The learning extensions one can engage in at this time provide a backdrop for scientific awareness skills that hopefully will last a lifetime!

In March we eagerly await the naughtiness that comes with the St. Patrick's Day shenanigans. Here again is a golden opportunity to prolong, sustain and view childhood the way it should be. Though the idea of characters the likes of leprechauns is foreign to many children, they are certainly still evident on one particular cereal box. Happily, six year olds are still amazed and satisfied to find a "pot of gold" that probably only contains candy. They are content with believing the tale and feel fortunate to be surprised and thrilled to harvest even a minuscule amount of green glitter. Happily, violence is not part of the modus operandi of these tiny characters. Sometimes the simplistic celebrations take on a life of their own and are forever etched in the minds and hearts of little children who sadly are expected to grow up sooner than is necessary!

Along with the appearance of spring comes the apparent reawakening of the illustrious P.T.A. Surely silent preparations have been ongoing throughout the winter in readiness for the spectacular event known as the Carnival! This is a surefire money-maker for the school. There are any number of games and booths set up to lure unsuspecting children to spend their parent's money during a four hour period on a Saturday in March. Authentically speaking one can find tickets, prizes, contests, food, and face painting to mention a few. However, the big draw still appears to be frolicking in the huge bouncing enclosure that is set up in the gym. Naturally there are crowds of people, lots of noise and anticipation over the prospect of adding a large sum of money to the P.T.A. coffers. Many parents volunteer to create and man the booths for what must seem like an eternity. A fun-filled day indoors on a generally springy Saturday usually yields exhausted parents, bowls of dead goldfish given as prizes and a mop-up job only slightly smaller than that of "Woodstock" in days of old!

In what seems like an ever increasingly short period of time we seem to surge headlong into the Passover/Easter rituals. Here again I truly believe in separating the observance of these very special holidays. I am always amazed at how the tiny egg, a symbol of rebirth appears in both of these celebrations.

Biblically and historically the stories surrounding both Passover and Easter are well suited for at least superficial study as the concepts contained therein can only serve to enlighten the next generation. Both holidays illustrate the power of those who lead. Sadly overt as well as hidden persecution has existed in all societies since the dawn of time, much to the detriment of humanity. The attempted almost total annihilation of whole groups of people plus the assassination of a simple preacher who advocated loving one's neighbor is part and parcel of the events history has recorded. The sooner children learn to focus on our sameness as opposed to our differences, the better will be the chances of establishing pockets of freedom and fairness in classrooms around the world!

By now everyone has begun to enjoy the warmer weather and longingly children prematurely drag out those treasured shorts worn the fall before. They shed their light jackets early and yearn to run free, to swim and enjoy some leisure time. It is about this time that I realize all too well that our days are numbered. Testing begins in earnest and the air is filled with a myriad of pre-closing activities.

Probably the long-awaited culminating celebration that occurs regularly every June is the fifth grade graduation, formerly reserved for sixth graders. For these upper classmen the actual ceremony follows a momentous excursion to New York City to attend a Broadway show and dinner. Naturally, the P.T.A. provides an evening party at school where dancing, games, food and fun signal the beginning of the end!

Graduation is definitely the most beautifully choreographed event that takes place in our school. It is so professionally produced, directed and executed that the elegance and significance of this celebration has to leave a lasting effect on all those present. The graduates are coached tirelessly and finally in their school career experience the kind of discipline that enables them to listen, respond and move as one unit with the grace and efficiency of an army battalion. The resulting display is very moving in its seemingly effortless execution, exuding an aura of simplicity and style befitting the serenity of the occasion!

One cannot possibly come away from viewing such an emotionally moving spectacle and not be proud of the growth realized by each child in our elementary school. A feeling of well-being seems to permeate the room in spite of the heat, the crowds, the unlikely setting and the many parents jockeying for positioning in order to capture the perfect picture. Somehow for that one hour all is right with education and the future of our world appears to be assured. You study the faces before you and notice a strange combination of innocence, shyness, confidence, fear, anticipation, pride, joy and the stylish youthfulness that comes from just being a child of the nineties living in the United States of America!

Graduation signals to all a time for advancement, the yearly "changing of the guard", the "passing of the baton", a carefully calculated movement up the educational ladder, where ever increasing demands for self-motivation, independent work habits and a mature social awareness will most probably determine future academic success or the lack of it! With all of this in mind it is easy to see that maintaining any kind of real composure is a task of enormous difficulty. I try to console myself with the idea that this rite of passage is a necessary ending, heralding the beginning of greater challenges to come!

As we all pack up, "close up shop", recharge and renew our bodies, minds and souls, let us keep in mind that all the celebrations we experience are meant to be happy occurrences built into our lives to give our time on earth greater meaning while hopefully elevating our psyches to the distinct possibility of achieving new heights, perhaps even in areas previously uncharted. No one knows when or where or even who will become the next Einstein, Mozart, DaVinci, Mother Teresa, Ghandi or Longfellow! Every child we encounter could light the world with a fire from a flame that you ignite by your enthusiasm, your example, your zest for life and the love you have for the global future of our world!

Celebrate each day, the big and small happenings, the simple and complex occurrences that added together make-up the body of experiences indelibly emblazoned in the minds of the citizens of tomorrow! Be a mirror of joy and there will be no telling how far your influence will be felt. Live and love with gusto!

Happily & hopefully yours,
Pat

Chapter 6

November 1st

Dear Kristen,

I guess it's about time to have a serious talk about first graders. "What could be serious about first graders?", you say. There really is so much to say about this adorable age group. So I guess I'll start at the beginning! That way we'll understand just why and how they got to where we see them today!

As infants and later toddlers we all had a definite curiosity about our environment. We strained to make sense out of the sights and sounds that continually passed by us. We had the urge to touch, investigate, sample, ingest and otherwise experience all that we could reach.

As our skills and confidence grew we took those crucial steps that would eventually lead to some limited independence and thus definite growth. We discovered language and developed a healthy respect for the spoken word and what mastery of this skill would gain for us. We even dabbled in the use of silence, gestures, grimaces, the dreaded temper tantrums and any form of communication that seemed to get our message across.

It was obvious to us early on that adults were generally quite attentive and responsive to our needs. This pleased us and built up within us strong feelings of self worth. We got used to having our needs met in a fairly regular fashion. Thus, good vibes concerning our world and our place in it became securely established in our minds. This panacea, however could not last forever.

In time we all would grow in physical strength and we would long to stretch our communication skills with our new found peers. These wondrous creatures just happen to be the same age we are. They enjoy similar things and they exhibit similar skills. However, we soon see that these positives don't necessarily out-weigh the negatives all the time. Sadly, we learn that our peers communicate as well as we do. They have nearly the same wants and needs we have. Worst of all, they want the things we want at precisely the same time and for just as valid reasons. Then too, they have adults around them who love and adore them as much as our families care for us. We also find that we have to deal with these new found playmates on a regular basis. At times they are so much fun to have around and at other times they frustrate us beyond belief. And so our world expands and becomes more complicated, just when we were getting used to it all!

Along the way, we all somehow mastered toilet training, haircuts, visits to the doctor and dentist, tooth brushing, confining shopping carts, distasteful babysitters, unwanted baths, skinned knees and going to bed. Then one day they tell us we have to go to school. And that's where teachers come in!

Up until this point life has been only mildly complicated. Now, things could be potentially quite frustrating as well. It seems that we are entering a world where two or three children become twenty or more.

We learn that louder or naughtier often gets the attention faster, even if that attention is negative in nature. We realize sooner or later that there are new rules in this big organization called, school. We meet competition and we sadly learn that we are constantly being evaluated and compared with our peers as well as our siblings. Worst of all, the many hours formerly reserved for all kinds of experimental play slowly disappears as we begin the task of formal education. Fun is now often relegated to the playground at recess or after school play-dates. Socialization, though encouraged is now a function of special rules concerning times and places. Spontaneity is often a thing of the past and make-believe isn't really totally acceptable anymore.

As children we learn to survive the perils of the lunchroom and the bus rides to and from school. We develop strategies to handle the bathroom, the separation from Mom, the playground, the locker room and the hallway. We find out that people are not always what they purport to be and there are even ways to get into trouble by one's sheer presence alone. We also find that how one looks and dresses, plus one's toys and other magical playthings can often determine popularity. In the early years it becomes obvious that being a good student is important to adults and even to peers. We learn a lot about disappointments and hurt feelings, loneliness and sadly even failure. There are times when we are enthralled with learning and other times when we are bored and totally unaffected. We agonize over our loss of freedom and the necessity to consider the welfare of others while striving to have our own needs met. We may even detest sharing time, love, attention and praise with so many others. All this we are required to do in the name of education!

And so this perhaps bouncing, bubbly first grader starts school in September armed with at least one year of experience in Kindergarten. As he or she picks out just the right outfit to wear on that momentous day, each child brings along the sum total of all their experiences to date. Some are confident that they have the whole "school" thing figured out. Others are scared of any new experience. The highly verbal child may be covering up all kinds of insecurities, while the shy one just needs to develop confidence. The naughty one could be just playful or he might be a product of imaginary or real failure in Kindergarten. Whatever the case, our task is just beginning!

Remember that six year olds are very much divided in their thinking as to their roles. Girls like the colors pink and lavender and still enjoy playing with dolls. Boys dabble somewhat seriously in sports, both as spectators as well as novice players. They are generally quite knowledgeable. However, despite this dichotomy both boys and girls have been known to play together, interact warmly and even develop sincere friendships over time. They are protective of each other and will champion the cause of a classmate and offer due praise fairly to both genders. Sadly, many will just as soon tattle on the very same person who was praised ten minutes earlier.

Six year olds are self- centered to be sure. They consider paper dropped on the floor to have a definite ownership. If asked to retrieve something that is not their possession, the average first grader will refuse resoundingly. However, this practice can lovingly over time be turned around. Kindness, thoughtfulness and compassion is very possible for six year olds to learn, but it takes time because that requires thinking about another person. It always amazes me that first graders are so bright in some ways and so seemingly unable to think in certain situations. A recurring theme has always baffled me. A youngster will proudly discover a staple, tack or scrap of paper on the floor and instantly want to know what to do with it. While the answer seems obvious to us, perhaps the training at home presents different possibilities to each individual child. First graders like precise answers and predictable routines. They function best in an orderly situation where fairness prevails. Often this age group is toughest on themselves. Most are painfully honest, but there are exceptions to this as well. They respond well to deserved praise and seem to flounder badly when scorned, embarrassed or treated negatively. I always make it a point to recognize growth in very detailed and personal ways. I recall openly how only a few weeks ago a certain child had such difficulty with a task that now seems easy. This impresses six year olds.

Since first graders are very social, it probably won't be a surprise to you to learn that they are often quite nosy. Some of them have the ability to overhear a quiet conversation twenty feet away. Others have the knack of always being in the right place at the time that some news is related. Still others are determined to interrupt every time someone is speaking, whether privately or otherwise. And it always amazes me just how many witnesses there are to absolutely anything that happens!

Call it curiosity, if you will! In any case six year olds are determined to find out how old their teachers are, what religion they are and if they are married. These are essential facts to most first graders. I think it is their attempt to feel and act grown-up. They love comparing notes on Hanukkah and Christmas. The general consensus in this area seems to be that Hanukkah is better. Naturally, eight days of presents beats only one. So much for the math program!

Generally speaking, first graders are quick to believe anything their teacher says. However, it often goes beyond that. Parents have reported that the teacher's word is "gospel". They have often complained to me that children have told parents that they don't explain things correctly. Lately, a little girl asked me if she could attend a late functioning show on a school night three months from now. I responded that the decision was one her parents must make. The child excitedly replied that the parents would accept my opinion in this case. Sometimes I wonder who my students really are!

Another surprising thing about first graders is how honest they usually are. They are generally convinced that it's better to tell the truth. Besides most of them are not adept at lying. There are always tell-tale signs that adults can readily see. In such situations you'll see how well developed some six year olds are at "prophetizing". They can recite every substantiating fact or moral that applies in any case pending. These mini-prophets are usually the exact ones who have committed the offense at another time. Therefore, this qualifies them as experts!

Happily, six year old boys play quite nicely. Just give them a ball and they have fun with few incidents. When boys become physical, however they get over it quickly and rarely hold grudges. They are highly competitive, but also love being part of a team. They don't get involved in excluding a prospective player and a leader soon assumes the role with general acceptance. Boys don't seem to care much about clothes at this age. They are quite happy in sweats and jogging suits. They are more interested in activity than in looks by and large. Boys love to figure out how things work and they are usually thinkers and problem solvers. Sadly, however boys are generally more immature than girls and thus they have a harder time adjusting to the rigors of school. Because they are generally more active, they are deemed harder to teach. I have always found boys to be excellent students. They really are willing to please and they are interested in a variety of things. If you change activities often and believe in the element of surprise, boys can enliven and enrich any classroom. Even the shy ones turn out to be noteworthy, because they often turn out to be the dependable and mature ones.

Girls, on the other hand are definitely more complicated. They learn early all about the wiles characteristic of our sex. It seems that these little females have "the word" passed on to them through some underground social pipeline. Namely, they learn that only certain girls are the right ones. These so called accepted females band together to exclude the others. Girls get involved in establishing ties that are too intense at this age. The first best friend and the second best friend and the third best friend could all be switched around or replaced in a day. Already, girls have difficulty with the distinction between acquaintances and friends. Then to, a group of three spells trouble if they are all girls. There is rarely peace in such a lopsided situation. Someone invariably gets hurt and generally it's the least dominant of the three! They fight about everything and often it's a secret that was revealed or some sensitivity type of infraction. You might say that these are budding teenagers and you're correct! However, all girls are not like this. There are still some unassuming girls who act and think appropriately, but each year there seems to be fewer of the so-called "old-fashioned" girls. It seems to me that the women's lib movement has finally filtered down to the six year old. Girls are very independent now and rarely show any fear of boys even when the latter are bigger in size. Girls have learned to use language as a defense and they are winning. Girls are still guilty of tattling more often than boys, but it also depends on the particular mix of children. Often it's the motive that is different. Boys are more interested in fairness, while girls are sometimes tattling to delight in seeing a peer being reprimanded.

Happily, there is still an element of wonder and fantasy in the minds and hearts of six year olds. They can grab onto an idea and carry it to many different conclusions. Some children are still able to believe in the highly illogical tale of Santa Claus. Others, while suspect seem to hold tenaciously to their belief, hoping that it's really true. It amazes me how cynical the unbelievers can appear. They spout their ideas loudly and confidently, almost in a scornful manner, anxious to add converts to their side of the issue. The same holds true for the "tooth fairy" tale and even the infamous leprechauns on St. Patrick's Day. Perhaps it takes the maturity of adults to enjoy these childhood tales in the way they were meant to be appreciated.

I mentioned earlier about the high esteem in which first graders hold their teachers. Well, in most instances, six year olds are also in awe of their older brothers, sisters, cousins or family friends. Secretly, they long to be BIG and they are often frustrated due to the fact that they cannot keep up or compete with these older counterparts. At times this becomes a real problem, especially when the siblings are of the same sex. What seems so logical to us, can be totally incomprehensible to a starry-eyed six year old.

Along these lines, it is easy to see that first graders could be impressed by learning difficult skills. Anything presented as a challenge is immediately appealing to them. They'll try almost anything to please and to be thought of as grown up. They also love responsibility in the form of going on errands around the school and getting homework for siblings and neighbors. They love to help in the classroom and are the best desk cleaners and book arrangers I've ever seen. No job is too tough, hard or heavy for even the slightly built first grader. Volunteers are available way before the task is even explained. Enjoy these traits, because they often disappear in the middle grades.

Happily, first graders are spontaneous! You never quite know what they will say in any given situation. They love being "on stage" in the classroom. Show and Tell suits them just fine. While it can turn into "bring and brag", it's quite easy to monitor Show and Tell if they understand the rules. Usually, the outspoken ones like to predominate, but this doesn't always transfer to acting out plays. Quite often the shy ones turn out to be the "stars"! First graders are not afraid to speak their minds, even when they aren't sure what the topic is really about. In an attempt to feel grown up, six year olds will often use language inappropriately. They are unaware of words with multiple meanings and so they often confuse concepts. However they have the animation and the need to express themselves in many ways.

These six year olds of today amaze me with their indomitable spirits and their zest for life. Some of them appear to fear nothing and no one. I remember how thoughts of seeing the principal conjured up all sorts of fears in my mind. Today's youngsters look upon the principal as a true pal. They easily approach him and want to relate all kinds of stories, particularly those involving peer misdemeanors. Using the principal as a threat doesn't seem to work the way it used to when I was a child. In the old days you never wanted to be sent to the principal's office. Now children are interested to see what it's like in there.

Happily, first graders are fearful of forgetting homework or library books. They want to conform and haven't really become individuals in the narrow sense of the word. Many six year olds are afraid of the negative things that occur daily on the bus. However, there are always first graders who initiate fisticuffs, teasing, horsing around and other deviant forms of behavior. Many of them are often modeling the behaviors of older children who also ride the bus.

Just remember that six year olds are at the crossroads. This year will either make or break them as students. If they become motivated, skilled and independent workers, they will be students for life! If they lose that zest for a life of learning, they will become mediocre students at best. Knowing how they function as a group and individually should help you to plan and present the curriculum in a way that is refreshing, appealing and concrete. In so doing your success and theirs is assured. I hope you come to love six year olds as I do. They have a positive view of life and boundless energy. Needless to say, first graders love whatever you try to do for them and happily they are not afraid or embarrassed to show their affection openly. I just know they'll get "under your skin". Enjoy them!

Warmly,
Pat

Chapter 7

November 4th

Dear Kristen,

It's the eve of the election, a crucial time to be sure. Choosing candidates to govern our great country is a responsibility not to be taken lightly. In years past presidential elections were events necessitating the closing of school. Today schools still are used as polling places, and I prefer seeing them open. That way children get the feeling of how the election privilege impacts on society as a whole. Needless to say, first graders are not too young to begin learning to appreciate the process by which we govern ourselves. The casting of one's vote is one of the ways we exercise our citizenship. A mock election is always an exciting way to help illustrate this yearly process. Besides it satisfies the competitive spirit most first graders display. They should have the beginnings of a superficial understanding of the composition of our country, namely that we are a group of fifty states, governed by various branches elected by the people. Children should know where the President resides and something about his responsibilities. While learning about classroom rules and village ordinances, children can readily appreciate the need for laws. They will also see that these laws must be monitored by people who are hired to protect our interests. It is always a good idea to continually impress upon youngsters the need to be readers. This lifelong activity impacts on every area of society and is a skill that one can never master completely.

So let's begin with this most complex skill and try to unravel its mystery. Most children begin or are taught the consonant sounds in Nursery School only to have them re-taught in Kindergarten. This sounds like an easy task, but remember that our language is not always regular. The letter "c" has no sound and therefore takes the sound of "k" or "s", etc. Then later on children are presented with consonant blends as in "tr" or vowel blends as in "ea" not to mention consonant digraphs like "th", plus vowel digraphs such as "ow" and "au" to further complicate matters.

I have always found it best to teach children a basic sight word list of about fifty simple words, plus the color and number words as a way to get them reading very elementary selections quickly. This is done through every kind of drill imaginable. At the same time, a heavy emphasis on beginning sounds must be coupled with an in-depth study of the short vowels beginning with "a". You see, vowels are the keys that unlock the word. Children who can decode well usually become excellent readers. They possess a solid sight base and can decode unfamiliar words using the phonetic skills taught in a sequential order. Consonants, short vowels, blends, and digraphs followed by repeating short vowels and adding endings 's', 'ed' and 'ing', plus 'ly', 'y', 'er', and 'es' give children a firm start. One should intermingle rhyming words and short vowel substitution, as well as an on-going list of compound words, synonyms and antonyms to enrich the fund of vocabulary children are able to read at any given time. Naturally, the development of sight words is an ever-growing process. A rich science and social studies curriculum can energize and enrich communication skills across the board. Environmental vocabulary so crucial to achieving a practical overall awareness including safety in our world is a necessity and should be constantly addressed.

In the second half of the year, the long vowels should be taught as well as the vowel patterns. Concurrently, the list of sight words taught should constantly be increased. The beginning color and number words can be modified to include more sophisticated samples, plus simple action words should be followed by all kinds of category words, namely words for people, descriptive words, words that name tools, furniture, sports, days of the week, months of the year, holiday words, school vocabulary, and even area street names etc. The list of categories is endless and provide children who are receptive with a colorful vocabulary which will serve them in good stead in writing as well as the reading area!

When a child is able to combine the knowledge of sight words with the ever increasing ability to decode phonetically, then and only then is there a chance for comprehension to occur. If a child spends an inordinate amount of time decoding words, then he or she is losing meaning, and the latter is surely the purpose for learning to read. For true comprehension brings enjoyment to the reading process. Without understanding, reading becomes a chore that has no apparent purpose for children. Then to, intuitive and literal skills cannot be strengthened and one can not hope to introduce or expect any kind of mastery over "cloze" skills, skimming or inferential skills. The resulting frustrations eventually cause children to give up because learning to read is perceived as too hard. Therefore, a strong phonetic ability is a crucial key to unlocking the code that we call reading!

Hopefully, children can become equally adept at both sight and phonetic methods of learning to read. However, more than occasionally, you meet a child who has difficulty with one or the other method. It therefore becomes necessary to instruct that child in his or her area of strength. This will help develop the confidence to continue advancing while the weaker area is attacked via other means.

As reading vocabulary builds, little short paragraphs can be introduced so that children have a chance to use their skills. Frequent re-reading may seem to promote memorization and often does, but this is really another form of drill and it is one in which children get a chance to "perform" and be heard by themselves as well as their peers. At the same time those same words are seen and spoken over and over again. Remember, reading is such a new skill for most first graders. It requires constant practice. To six year olds, learning to read English is like learning any foreign language would be for each of us adults! It is difficult, complex, filled with rules and often frustrating. Here is where another skill becomes important.

I'm sure you realize that the more verbal a child is, generally the better reader and writer he or she becomes. The reason is that highly verbal children usually possess excellent speaking vocabularies. They know the names of the articles in our world. They can think of other names for the same thing. They understand multiple meanings of words, sayings and expressions. This knowledge gives them a definite edge. In short they can communicate effectively and so they learn to use context clues automatically. They read picture clues easily and quickly. They anticipate motives, inferences and can predict what the characters might do in any given situation and they can also predict outcomes that are consistent with the story line. Generally, these children have vivid imaginations and are never at a loss for words. All of these skills aid in the quest for meaning.

As the year progresses and the materials read become more and more challenging, children should have repeated practice in locating factual and other supporting clues in paragraphs. They should be able to prove via concrete evidence the difference between fact and opinions. They should be able to distinguish between fact and fantasy and they should be able to adequately come up with the main idea of a paragraph as well as summarize the important ideas of a book without divulging the punch line or the ending. They should also be able to identify the moral of a story and reword it in their own fashion. You might be thinking that all of the above is really "a tall order" for first graders. Remember that we are basically exposing children to these complex skills as they are ready to assimilate them. There will probably always be a group of youngsters who will not be able to handle such advanced skills until second grade or beyond. In such cases it becomes necessary to guard against damaging often fragile self images. Repeated gentle encouragement and heartfelt praise can go a long way to bolster self-confidence and ease nervousness. How easy it is to underestimate the enormity of the task learning to read is for young children!

On the other side you're bound to encounter the precocious child who is advanced compared to his peers. Early screening of all children helps to identify the emergent readers and prevent the kind of boredom that can lead to disciplinary problems. Essentially, you must set up individualized activities commensurate with the level of instruction shown on each child's individual test results. A separate reading folder filled with challenging activities carefully explained and ordered can go far toward giving you the crucial time needed to work with the average and low end youngsters in a small group setting.

Placing children in homogeneous reading groups as soon as possible is crucial in order to give them a sense of movement curriculum-wise. They should often be exempt from some of the vocabulary sessions that are necessary for the bulk of the class. That way you can begin to foster a sense of independence, maturity and creativity in the approximate top third of the class without frustrating the remainder of the children. Subtly these precocious children must feel that because they are currently advanced, more will be expected of them. Naturally, you must make them feel special by continually requesting that they earn the privilege of further advancement. Always be on the look-out to establish, encourage and maintain neatness of written work, organization of materials and proper social behavior during independent work periods. Frequent praise and recognition of all kinds spur children to do more. Otherwise, you run the risk that the enriched work will be perceived as a punishment for being so-called "smart"! You see there is a delicate balance that must be carefully observed and refined in order to provide an environment conducive to optimum success for every child.

Large group instruction is a key component to any reading program, because it is in this forum that new skills are presented to the bulk of the class. The upper third must reprove that they have mastered such skills in order to continue enrichment activities. Average and low end readers having just been exposed to a new skill are reminded that these same skills will be repeated in the near future. Somewhere along the continuum each child will hopefully attain the desired skills. Both mental and written notes must be copiously kept to insure that no child is being passed over.

Just like a construction engineer, you must build your reading foundation carefully from the ground up. Your "cement mixture" must contain equal parts of phonetic skills, plus a strong sight word base and structural analysis skills, not to mention an ever increasing speaking vocabulary, a high degree of repetition, frequent modeling experiences and daily "immersion" in all types of rich and varying literature!

What materials are best equipped to address the recipe stated above? The answer resoundingly is a diverse variety of all types of genre featuring colorful vocabulary depicting fascinating and believable stories about topics of interest to young children. Basal texts are NOT the demons some educators make them out to be!!! How any material is perceived by the teacher responsible for disseminating the information contained therein, is the only crucial element here. Basal texts provide the security of well ordered skills using a controlled vocabulary. This enhances and strengthens the glue already injected. Literature anthologies, Big Books, weekly children's newspapers and all other library materials can creatively supplement any basal reading series and add life to a tried and true method of reading instruction.

In conclusion, no one really knows how or exactly when the multitude of reading skills become second nature to a child and knowledge seeking takes on a life of its own. As learned as we are, no educator can adequately explain how or when one becomes secure in "cracking the code". Therefore, we must "cover all the bases" expending all our collective energies using every known method and all the materials at our disposal to be sure that all children have a fair shot at a secure start in reading!

Similarly, we must realize that the reading-writing connection is a strong one and that verbal expression, grammar, English, handwriting and spelling must function in conjunction with the orderly presentation of reading skills.

It is crucial to use the basic sight vocabulary built in September and October to concurrently teach the concepts of plurals, punctuation, sentence construction, action words, pronouns, synonyms, antonyms, compound words, category words and the like. These skills directly influence growth in creative writing as well as inventive spelling. It should be easy to see that the sum total of the Language Arts program is made up of many components that hang together for dear life. A weakness in any area mentioned above creates stress and a loss of reading comprehension and/ or less than average communication using the written word.

In the early stages children are encouraged to independently stretch out the sounds in the words they are attempting to spell, thereby creating written communication through the vehicle of "invented" spelling. Process writing advocates have had great success in using this tactic to give children license to write without worrying about correct spelling. I agree with this idea to a point. In the initial stages all writers like to experience the free-flow of ideas. However, somewhere along the line all "finished" pieces need to be edited or the publishing process cannot take place. Realistically speaking I have found that even children as young as first graders are hungry to know the correct spelling of words. They delight in being able to spell accurately and those who have photographic memories or excellent auditory skills will remember many words on a first exposure. Then why not teach but not require perfect spelling on rough drafts?

By now you probably have the idea that reading and allied subjects are of paramount importance in the first grade curriculum. I'm sure you realize that the Language Arts program takes up a good portion of each and every day. You are absolutely right. However, just remember that science and social studies are wonderful ancillary subjects. They provide the themes around which you can build your reading, writing, spelling and English skills. The fascinating topics of weather, plants and animals, planets, health & safety, simple machines, and a host of experiments serve to enrich the speaking and reading vocabularies of children while exploring topics that are certainly most interesting to children of this age.

Science is a subject that should never be taught as an extra. It is a hands-on course of study that is current and abounds in every facet of our lives. Science is a core curriculum subject that is eye-catching and totally appealing to the native curiosity of six year olds, boys and girls alike. The elements of surprise and wonder follow from predictions on topics that can be explored on various levels. Where would we be without the glorious triumphs directly related to science that have occurred over the years? Our very lives depend on the creation of future scientists who have the stamina, the dedication and the patience to explore uncharted waters in search of cures, improvements and advances that will enrich all of our lives. Every renowned scientist began his or her career as a first grader filled with wonder at the mysteries of our planet! Bravo!!

Similarly, as humans we are first and foremost social beings. We prefer living in groups for safety, pleasure and for the continuance of the species. Therefore, we are charged with learning how to effectively live together, govern ourselves and pursue our own individual dreams while leading rich rewarding lives in peace and harmony with the animal and plant kingdoms with whom we share our earth. This is no small task. The history of the world is replete with wars, persecution and injustices of all kinds. In studying other cultures we hope to caution future generations not to repeat the mistakes of the past. First graders can begin the democratic process by drafting class rules and establish a rotating system for the performance of jobs etc. Calendar studies as well as experiencing holidays and traditions give children a sense of our culture and its values. Primitive map studies begin to acquaint children with representing the world in manageable "bites" that are more easily digestible. They must begin to understand the role of geography in the history of the world. Current events, newspaper articles and the like bring the world into the classroom and embellish vocabularies, Show and Tell topics and simple report topics. As with science, social studies is a core curriculum area filled with fascinating concepts that can be woven into poetry, biographies and the like. It is crucial for children to have some sense of who they are and where they came from so that they will be further armed with the knowledge and the skills necessary to become the educated citizens of tomorrow. The safety and security of our great country depends on the first social steps of our youngest citizens!

Certainly, as you've no doubt noticed, everything taught in first grade is crucial! Math is no exception! Wonderfully logical math is so often maligned by teachers who find it cut and dried and so project it in that manner. They proceed page by page in workbooks without any thought to making math the creative subject that it is. Sadly math is often intimidating to girls in the later years. Why is this? Perhaps girls see it as a masculine subject ! It could also be that some girls need to be taught math a different way. In any case, anxiety at a young age can block any child's normal math development. How sad to think that some children never discover the inherent wonder in the orderly progression of numbers and the variety of mathematical operations all related and interesting in and of themselves.

Young children have an inborn natural curiosity about numbers and counting. First graders are impressed with the concept of infinity and they drool over writing "big" numbers, feeling grown-up and highly capable. Beginning with the concrete, one should move slowly progressing to the abstract in each mathematical area so that understanding will not be compromised.

Happily at this level children who tend to struggle

with reading skills could have a chance to shine in math. Catching the math spirit is crucial now, before reading skills impact on math ability, namely when the word problem makes its appearance. This is the time to play endless rote games to insure the memorization of math facts. Learning to think mathematically and logically starts on day one! Once understanding is assured math facts must be committed to memory. We have far too many adults who can't function in math. We cannot afford to continue in this vein.

First graders naturally grapple with money concepts, because they have far too few opportunities to use money in the real world. Suburban youngsters have no independence and their exposure to situations calling for the use of money is limited. When given a twenty dollar bill to spend at the P.T.A. Book Fair, most children have no clue as to how many books they might purchase or how much change they are due.

On the other hand, I never cease to be amazed at the depth of knowledge one can extract from first graders if one continually focuses on the relationships depicted in numeration for example. It is critical to make math the exciting subject that it is. Math is inherently motivating if it is taught properly. I usually teach math after lunch when we all need some sheer excitement. Cooperative learning works well in the teaching of math skills. That way the shy, insecure and unsure child can benefit from the group's efforts and over time develop confidence. Math is an action packed, colorful and entirely engaging subject that lends itself to a variety of approaches. I find it the subject that allows me to "let my hair down" and get right into it!

In September I begin with the study of the comparison signs; equal, not equal, greater than and less than, weaving the pictured sets, numerals, and number words into the concept to add difficulty. Then I approach the operation of addition in every way with daily drill and finally returning to the comparison terms and using them in addition. By November, I attack the missing addend concept as well as subtraction, showing in every way the relationships that exist therein. In January, I plunge headlong into numeration and place value in an attempt to rename and define the numbers from ten to one hundred. Included in this time frame are the simple addition and subtraction of two and three digit numbers. I joyfully teach expanded notation and counting by twos, threes, fours, fives, sixes, sevens, eights, nines and tens starting from any number!!!

In the spring we approach telling time, fractions, geometry, measurement, and money according to the math curriculum I've outlined in the appendix. In May and June I try to introduce multiplication, carrying and borrowing, Roman numerals and the idea of negative numbers. Needless to say, computer studies, graphing, numeral dictation, timed math tests and word problem development has been on-going!

All too soon the math period is over and my sense of satisfaction is complete. Math is the "gym class of the academic setting"! It's a chance to kick up one's heels and express real joy in learning! Math is visual, tactile, and concrete. Success in life depends on developing a secure math sense as well as a growing problem solving ability! Immerse your youngsters in all that is mathematical on an impromptu basis and soon a math sense will become almost second nature! Enjoy!

Hopefully, you have realized that the first grade

curriculum is fully packed with both basic as well as challenging skills. It behooves us all to see that each child feels a sense of movement along the curriculum path in all areas. That way an inner motivational spirit can take over and serve to spur each child on according to his own time frame. With hard work, endless energy, creativity and lots of love each child can feel a measure of success that will give them positive vibes regarding education and make them true lifelong learners. It is to this end that we are daily challenged!

Always,
Pat

Chapter 8

November 12th

Dear Kristen,

Well, sooner or later it was bound to happen. Report cards are upon us, the dreaded vehicle "we" use to determine the academic progress and well being of each of our students. At this time of year I always feel like a henchman of sorts, a doctor determining health or illness or a judge who issues an edict on the guilt or innocence of the accused. The parallel is really quite accurate if you think about it.

These bouncy, bubbly six year olds that I spoke of earlier are at the threshold of something really big. Everyone in their lives to date has attempted to convey the idea that they are simply wonderfully unique creatures destined for stardom in life! Then we come along with a piece of paper, called a report card that could change all the positive vibes an impressionable youngster has heretofore received. I hate this age old practice!

Elementary school should be a time of positive growth and challenges with high standards to be sure, but with narrative reports that resemble the current I.E.P. descriptions used for special education students. The vague grading system used by most school districts leaves little to be desired as far as painting an accurate picture of a child. It is exceedingly difficult and definitely quite subjective to decipher the difference between satisfactory, good, or excellent at a time when children are just beginning the educational process. I constantly fear the psychological damage that could take place at this crucial juncture.

School boards, administrators, parents and teachers alike are obviously concerned with accountability and rightly so. However, steadily progressing students are born of excellent teachers who motivate, teach and model a thirst for knowledge that is infectious!!! A talented teacher who is organized and in daily touch with a child's oral and written work, will never allow a student to slide. When parents are informed weekly of a child's progress in all areas, there is little need for a seasonal report card which can pass on bad news long after a negative pattern has been established.

Quarterly face to face parent conferences would be far superior to anything written. Such meetings would serve the purpose of cementing the dialogue between parents and the school. More importantly, the whole child could be discussed, taking in social, emotional, physical as well as academic concerns. Appropriate testing and work samples could be shared in a meaningful way. Proposals for improvement could be mutually drawn up and agreed upon and the parent would go home with a feeling of well being and a measure of security and confidence in the educational process, rather than a host of meaningless letters and or numerals which inadequately describe any human being!

Standardized tests have always been used to measure the progress of individual children as well as give some indication of the success of teachers, not to mention comparing classes, schools , districts and states. These, however are a feeble attempt to "play policeman". Since these tests measure large numbers of youngsters, I have always found them to be skewed to the median of the class. There is very little that is challenging on these tests and therefore the results don't really give you an accurate picture of anything beyond minimal proficiency. To be sure, the results of district testing is published for all the surrounding communities to reflect upon, compare and in some cases agonize over. However, when you factor in all the variables and the level of competency expected, you realize that a child does not have to answer very many questions correctly in order to pass with flying colors. It all adds up to great P.R. for the district.

Similarly, the fifth grade writing test is mostly graded on creativity and content, with little regard to mechanics. It seems that since the advent of "whole language" instruction, coupled with "spell check" on computer programs, spelling, grammar and punctuation have been pushed into the background and perhaps left there to die a natural death! So much for measurements such as these that tend to give one an unrealistic picture of a child's capabilities in writing.

Therefore, with all of the above in mind it behooves us to be as accurate as possible in our assessment of each child's progress. There are two schools of thought on this topic. One is that teachers should measure a child against himself. So a child of average intelligence who is categorized as learning disabled, but who is making steady progress could conceivably receive an "A" in reading. The other theory is that each child should be measured against whatever is considered average for a child of the particular grade. In that case, individual differences are not taken into account and each child is graded according to what he achieves.

Thus according to the example given above, the L.D. child would probably never earn an "A" grade. It all comes down to the services rendered. If a child is seen by the resource teacher and has been granted a modified curriculum, then it is conceivable that documented and mutually agreed upon special arrangements for such a youngster could merit that child an "A" grade.

Another hidden type of problem with the topic of accountability is that each adult who works with a child motivates and responds to him differently. Therefore, it often happens that two people see or perceive a child in opposing ways. There are many stories of children who progress beautifully with one teacher and who conversely do poorly or less well with another person. It all comes down to the perception the teacher develops of the child. If a child is seen as lazy and unmotivated, then that is the behavior that child will exhibit. If one perceives a child to be alert, alive, and bright, then that youngster will have a better chance of success. By now you have probably guessed that the self-fulfilling prophecy is at work! You bet it is, every day in every classroom world wide!

To be sure, one cannot be naïve enough to say that the self-fulfilling prophecy is the only variable having a bearing on accountability. However, one cannot leave this topic without seriously stating that in the end, the success or failure of each child is more dependent upon the adults whom he encounters, than on the child himself! You see, I believe that we, the teachers and parents are solely accountable for the progress of each child. Unless there are limiting factors, such as serious physical, emotional, or social defects, all children should be able to achieve to the extent that they are capable and at least attain minimum competency. It is the responsibility of all adults to motivate, model and teach the lessons of life pertinent to a child's level of understanding. Further, we are charged to deepen, strengthen and continually expand the horizons of each child so that "the sky's the limit" is an expression which can describe the future potential of every child placed in our care. The environment and the excitement we create in our classrooms and at home should be a constant source of delight for children. They should never cease to be amazed at the lessons they are exposed to and the varying ways they are challenged to beat their personal best!

Our future depends on the talents we perfect and the infectious love of learning we bring to each youngster. In the end our accountability must be measured more by these standards and less by the results of man-made tests that are either skewed socially, academically or mathematically! One doesn't have to be a Ph.D. to know if a teacher is gifted and children are inspired! Perhaps one day we will grow to the realization that accountability should be inherently entwined in the philosophy of educators and parents alike. It should be a silently understood thread in the fiber of our educational system. Never should we have to expose it for all to see, for in so doing, we undermine our purpose and lower the teaching profession to a level that is not befitting such a noble career! Accountability is for all of us, all the time, whenever and wherever we touch, mold, teach and care for humanity! This is my belief!!!

May it always be yours!

Confidently,
Pat

Chapter 9

December 10th

Dear Kristen,

Well, it's that time again! The holiday crunch is upon us and if you are anything like the rest of us, you are already bemoaning the lack of time to shop. This hectic time of year requires the " patience of a saint " and the fortitude of a long distance runner! So this might be the perfect time to entertain the topic of Organization and Planning!!!

Perhaps you are wondering why I waited until now to approach this crucial subject. As it turns out everything involved with teaching is deemed crucial in my book. I just felt that you needed some time to "get your feet wet"! Adjustments should always be ongoing and good teachers are continually re-evaluating their programs, methods and materials in order to facilitate learning.

Organization is basic to the operation of any business or enterprise. Running a classroom is very similar to organizing a household, a hospital or a luxury liner. The head of the operation must have a down - to - earth sense of practicality, a real flair for the creative, the instincts of foraging mammals, a superior sense of timing and the combined talents of an architect, an interior designer, and a cleaning service engineer!

Setting up a classroom is one of the first tasks that one must undertake. It is a purely individualized process, depending on your personality and the grade you teach. However there are some universal hints or guidelines that might assist you in the ever changing design of your classroom.

Naturally, the type of furniture you are given has a great bearing on the design arrangement. Desks that are nailed to the floor, though less frequently seen now, are most definitely a restricting factor. Tables of varying shapes as well as movable desks provide a kind of flexibility that can add to your program.

Keep in mind that those bouncy first graders generally come to us with under- developed listening skills in most instances. They need to be continuously focused on YOU in order to learn. Arranging desks in clusters at the beginning does facilitate cooperative learning, but hinders their ability to focus on you as the leader! I strongly

suggest that for the first marking period at least, children should all face the blackboard so that they are better positioned to listen effectively. Also, concepts of right and left are more easily demonstrated when everyone is starting from the same vantage point.

File cabinets, rolling carts, extra tables etc. should be placed away from traffic areas so that they are accessible to all while fulfilling a definite academic need. Many teachers employ activity centers where different subject materials are housed and used. This must be decided on when setting up your classroom.

It also helps to be a collector. Primary teachers are notorious for finding bargain items in large quantities in so called junk shops. They have collections of buttons, ribbon, spools, twine, yarn, paper plates, cardboard trays, pipe cleaners, decorations etc. They are adept at attending fire sales, rummage sales, and scouting bargains at flea markets all over the world. They are skilled at extracting donation items from stores, businesses, organizations and the like. These treasured items are stored in basements, playrooms, closets and garages of all creatively-minded teachers. These items eventually become part of many classrooms and are lovingly known as the "stock and trade" of elementary teachers everywhere.

Realistically when in the classroom you must also be aware of the outlets in the room, especially if you are placing a computer, fish tanks or other aids requiring electricity. Even the window placement is a necessary component, because accompanying curtains, blinds or verticals must be opened enough to allow light, but not so much that blackboard glare occurs. The latter can make it impossible for children to see adequately.

Surprisingly perhaps is the thought process involved in the placement of the teacher's desk. In days of old the teacher's desk was prominently displayed at the front of the room, denoting the adult's superiority and control. In those days a teacher spent most of his or her time lecturing and therefore the front was probably a logical place for the desk. However, the side or rear of the room works well when the teacher spends little time there. I use my desk as a place to keep student files, attendance records and my office supplies. I never sit at my desk. Therefore, it is not necessary to place my desk in active learning areas.

Remember that movable furniture makes it possible for you to change the arrangement of the room as maturity, curriculum and desire dictates. Don't be afraid to experiment. Children need and desire changes, especially if they are given solid reasons why the organization is being modified.

Always allow for the feasibility of the movement of traffic throughout the room. Provide a space to line up and a meeting area where discussions and the like can take place. Be sure that all furniture is away from the closet or "cubbie" area and that the sink section is isolated.

The blackboard is usually a focal point in the room unless it is a small free-standing one. It is wise to keep that area free so that children can see and use this age old tool to the fullest!

Once the furniture is physically placed, one can attack the curriculum accordingly. This part of organization is loosely termed, planning!

Planning involves many things, but basically it involves outlining the various curriculum topics in order from the simplest skill areas to the more complex ones. Planning is also the term given to the consideration of the objectives to be focused on, the materials used, the various methods employed and the timing and evaluation of the whole process. It's a "tall order" to say the least, but definitely one of the crucial elements a teacher must deal with on a daily basis.

Naturally, planning also depends heavily on the daily schedule that one is given. Usually the time schedule is not a negotiable item. The children have a set time for lunch, a special area subject as well as definite starting and ending times for each day. It's a well known unwritten law that the teaching of reading is the recommended way to start a primary child's day. Supposedly, children are "fresh" in the morning and thus more receptive to this fundamental area of instruction. I take opposition to this idea. I don't think it really matters one way or another which subject is first. It's more important to follow a quiet activity with a more active one. I also believe that all teacher directed lessons should be taught before independent activities can be approached. Actually, I do all language related subjects first and save the teaching of reading in groups for the end of the day when quiet activities involving drill and review are presented. Math and science are taught either directly before or following a special subject or lunch. That way a break occurs adjacent to the excitement of two fascinating areas of study. Again, one can not over emphasize the idea that the teacher's enthusiasm is a key factor in teaching any subject. The time of day is not a noteworthy variable!

Also, a very important consideration in planning is to always employ the spiral approach to teaching all subjects. This means that you teach a simple skill and then a succession of more complicated ones which hinge upon the simplest skill. In effect you always refer to the easier skill, thereby it is continually reviewed and embellished upon. For example, in phonics you teach the initial and final consonant sounds before the blends and digraphs. Medial consonant sounds can be delayed for a time because they are harder to hear and identify. Similarly, short vowels are generally found in three letter words. Mastering these sounds comes before the long vowels, which are generally easier to hear but are found in longer words.

In curriculum planning it is very helpful to study the subject guides from different companies and list the skills taught in Kindergarten, first and second grade. That way you will be able to appreciate the continuum that exists both before and after the grade level you teach. This also affords you the opportunity to review the skills previously taught. Thus this process gives you a more composite view of the skill continuum over time.

Plan books are the written vehicle used to keep one on target. Though specific in nature, weekly plans need constant updating. So much of teaching comes under the realm of feeling. It may be time for a particular lesson, but something tells you to do a different activity. Then by all means change the plan. Perhaps the children are not really ready for the next skill in the math sequence. If more review is indicated, then that must take place. Remember that each class is different and each child must be taken into consideration when you execute your plans. Then to, just because you have taught a skill, there is no guarantee that all of the children have processed it enough to be able to try the task independently. You may have to approach the same skill in many different ways before it actually can be used or mastered. A creative teacher knows a dozen ways to teach, depict or explain simple addition, which was taught in the fall. Two digit addition is basically a review of simple addition plus the concept of tens and ones.

The teaching of creative writing is a difficult one indeed. It runs parallel with the physical act of handwriting. The latter is often sabotaged, because of the bad habits that have been established to date. Usually toddlers begin writing skills with crayons improperly positioned. Nursery schools often allow all writing tools to be used without any instruction on proper handling. Therefore, we are handicapped in teaching the skills of letter formation because bad habits previously established are often impossible to break.

It is essential that the skills of creative writing be taught both by example, and in large, small and individualized settings. To simply say that a sentence begins with a capital letter means nothing to a child unless it is constantly repeated and shown individually during editing sessions. Sharing pieces provides an opportunity for children to offer constructive criticism, a chance to listen with a purpose and a means to showcase examples of skills to be emphasized. This kind of process writing is necessary in all grade levels and should be planned for on a regular basis.

A crucial thought to keep in mind is the idea that effective teachers have always known and that is - TEACH TO THE TOP OF THE CLASS! After you have your skills in each subject area ordered in your mind, remember that your timing and pace, besides your methods and materials are the most important aspects to be addressed. If you lose the top third of the class through boredom, you will only add prospective discipline problems to your roster. The average children always survive when stimulated. They will need repetition to be sure, but that is normal procedure. The lower third of the class always needs extra help, but without the stimulation of the faster learners, these needy youngsters usually become at best mediocre students. Don't allow that to happen. All children need huge amounts of love to reach their personal best. A smile, a pat on the back, and or a properly timed comment will carry a youngster further in his or her quest for academic proficiency.

Remember that each child needs to feel good about the day's accomplishments. I feel that it is essential to review the learnings of the day so that youngsters have a sense of what actually happened academically and what areas of growth have taken place over time. This gives them a feeling of purpose and a real perspective of achievement. Even if the day went poorly as sometimes happens, discussing the events along with collective brainstorming and problem solving will go far in shaping future days.

In any case, put each child on the bus with a smile and a good word. This practice will seal the end of the day's events and insure that the new day will start fresh with a clean slate upon which to record new experiences and forge new educational paths to academic proficiency and future self - actualization! That is our awesome task! That is our challenge! Plan and organize creatively, lovingly and thoughtfully and you will achieve a large measure of success!

Lovingly,
Pat

Chapter 10

January 4th

Dear Kristen,

Welcome to the almost second half of the school year! I hope you are well rested from the bustling holidays and ready to begin anew!

By now you have seen some children making great strides, while others continue to plod along or slowly lag behind. It's time to re-evaluate our goals, organization, teaching methods and individualization techniques. You see this is the time of year when those youngsters who were "sitting on the fence" begin to truly "take off". As the teacher you are the producer, director, stage coordinator, artistic designer, public relations person, and chief motivating force! Therefore, it is incumbent upon you to communicate daily in clear precise language the answers to what is being taught, to whom the lessons are directed and why the knowledge you are proposing to impart is important. Naturally, you must be well versed in various ways to teach each lesson so that optimum learning takes place.

To accomplish the above it is crucial for you to be the conductor or manager of a full-proof system of organization. For I believe that success in education largely hinges on the management system in effect in a classroom!

To start, one must have memorized the skills for each subject area in order from simplest to complex. These skills must be taught and re-taught in a spiral approach over time, weaving them into the content areas while increasing the difficulty of the overall material.

Daily routines and discipline also impact on the progress of your management system. Homework must be clear, organized and predictable as well as a review of material previously taught. Children must be well - versed in the answers to the following: "Who helps or doesn't help with written homework?", "Who signs or doesn't sign homework?", "How long should homework take?", "Where is homework placed when returned the following day?" "Is homework corrected with each child, corrected by the teacher or evaluated by peers?" Also an accurate accounting of the return and quality of homework as well as the mastery of skills presented should be kept in your grade book.

Weekly evaluations in sight vocabulary development, phonetic analysis and dictation skills as well as spelling and handwriting should consist of teacher made tests which are recorded and sent home weekly so that parents are constantly aware of the progress their children are making. Since all classwork is corrected and returned weekly, the communication lines remain open and strong. Then too, parents are being educated concerning the inner workings of a practical management system, one that they can emulate at home if need be!

The development of writing skills can be facilitated through informal mini-lessons given at least three times per week. As children attempt journal writing and other formal and informal writing tasks, a handy clipboard with children's names on a grid can provide a vehicle whereby teachers can jot notes concerning the strengths and weakness observed on a particular day. These notes form a written map to help guide the development of skills in a logical progression. Evaluation at report card time becomes an easier task if pertinent notes are kept and reviewed with parents.

Reading development should be checked upon completion of each book presented so that an accurate measure of skill development can be indicated quarterly. Such tests could be teacher-made or provided by the reading program used in the district. Certainly, an average level generalized test should be given quarterly to determine whether minimum competency has been achieved up to that particular point. Despite the fact that some children are functioning below the average at the time, you need to be able to demonstrate that such a youngster is in need of additional help, an alternate program or a total re-revaluation.

Similarly in math a teacher-made test could be given as topics are rotated. I typically test the concepts of set numeration to twenty using pictures and sight number words along with concepts of equal and unequal sets, and the comparison of sets that are greater than or less than each other as shown with pictorial clues and also in abstract form. The results of this test are placed in the child's class test folder and saved for parent conferences and report card grading. I then proceed to the topic of addition while also weaving the comparison terminology discussed above into the addition operation! No topic or skill in any area is ever abandoned or considered totally mastered in grade one!

While all the subject areas are taught on a daily basis, one should be able to spot the management system in operation; silently doing the job it was designed to do. It is to provide an efficient means for children to operate in a classroom so that they can maximize the learning of skills. These will then lead to comprehension, problem solving and the attainment of higher level thinking skills!

In order for this to happen consistently children must be organized and routinized in such a way that their predictable movements about the classroom are automatic and appear second nature. Examples of this are: knowing where to place completed independent work, demonstrating knowledge of expected behavior during small group instruction, showing efficient use of time, being able to store all notebooks, textbooks, folders, writing and drawing tools in the appropriate places, and being completely aware of rules for sharpening pencils, class participation, visiting the bathrooms, and procedures for pull-out classes, late arrival, assemblies, lining up, use of the closets and fire drill exercises.

When the above are in place, a solid working environment is created whereby the teacher's authority is established and the activities of the day move along in an orderly fashion. This facilitates the conditions necessary for creative learning!

Also, a well -trained class moves in unison the way an army battalion functions. Each person contributes to the well-being of the whole and thus productivity increases. Remedial teachers, special area personnel and substitute teachers also have a better chance of tapping into a management system that is already in place. For these ancillary personnel time is of the essence. They see children for a shorter amount of time and need to maximize their efforts. Cooperative learning heavily depends on the ability of youngsters to listen and "bounce off" each other. When the training and management system are in place, discipline remains in check and teachers can concentrate on the actual attainment of necessary skills, thus facilitating progress!

By now, perhaps you can see that the management system is one highly effective tool that the creative, disciplined and conscientious teacher begins to "train in" starting on day one! Teachers are solely responsible for the progress or lack of it for every child placed in their care! Just like the C.E.O.'s of every major corporation, success or failure of the company rests on his or her shoulders. So are we accountable for the education of our children. Our goal over twelve years is to create happy, highly-skilled citizens who are well on their way toward self-actualization! In business, profits are measured by the money that is made in selling an inanimate object or service. The C.E.O. is directly responsible to the stockholders as the government official's re-election is determined by how well he or she has served the constituency in question. Surely, the cause we seek to serve is of a higher nature and demands the kind of serious concentration to detail befitting the task.

Therefore, it behooves each of us to expend considerable thought and effort into developing and establishing a management system that we can live with and which serves the goals we have outlined for the children under our care!

Remember that children patterned by efficient managers will have a better chance of becoming organized and skilled students, not to mention the possibility of each of our children using these techniques personally later in life as they begin to choose careers and organize their lives. The need for management tools and skills is inherent in all "walks of life". When established early in the year, reviewed periodically and praised often, the management system can be the silent partner of a highly creative and effective teacher! This is a great time to check your management system and make "repairs" if necessary.

Happy New Year, Kristen! Each of us has the opportunity to start anew, "turn over a new leaf" or hang on to the status quo! Our children are counting on our educated decisions in all things. Take the time now! You won't be sorry!

Devotedly,
Pat

Chapter 11

February 8th

Dear Kristen,

Winter is surely upon us, despite what the Ground Hog "says" or does! During this generally indoor and reflective time it would do well for all of us as educators to consider the topic of dead, dying and/or lost subjects in our primary and intermediate curricula and beyond! Why, you say? Well, sometimes the cause of educational innovation bounds along at break-neck speed, picking up ancillary subjects and in the process "the tried and true" are often left to decay by the wayside! Perhaps this would be a good time to investigate this phenomenon and reconsider the merits of going "back to the basics"!

By now you have surely realized that the over-riding primary focus of first grade instruction is the effective teaching of reading! Naturally, this is a main concern, for a child's future educational progress depends heavily on the comprehension skills that come from excellent phonetic, literal, study and intuitive skills. However, parents in some cases still bemoan the gnawing question, " Why can't Johnny read?"

Over the years the educational pendulum has swung back and forth between the sight word enthusiasts versus the proponents of the phonetic approach in the teaching of reading. Also, we were alerted to the visual mode of learning, versus the auditory and tactile or kinesthetic modes. Periodically, the educational bandwagon purports to have discovered the one sure way to teach reading. Then we are all encouraged to jump blindly "on board" and seemingly experiment with our children, who in reality have only one chance to be first graders involved in beginning the process of learning to read. Even though the skill of reading is continued throughout life, the tone set at the beginning largely determines the progress made in the future. For some children a difficult start is a "turn off" that often cannot be repaired.

It seems to me that some words are phonetically correct and should be taught in that mode for children who hear sounds. When presented with words like "what" or "one", we have no choice but to memorize the configuration by sight. Bearing in mind that one cannot possibly learn the multitude of vocabulary words that exist by sight, it behooves us to consciously teach the phonetically regular words like "hat" and "plum" by the sounding out method and attempt by rote and otherwise to teach the many phonetic rules that apply as well as the exceptions to the rule. Children who gain a solid grasp of phonics early in their educational program and can add the crucial study of vowels to their decoding skills repertoire will undoubtedly meet success and become instant lovers of reading! Phonics is often bypassed as a legitimate area of study and millions of children over the years have been denied the benefit of learning this very old and previously respected skill. No reading program is complete without the study of phonics. However, sadly even today it still seems to be on the "endangered species list", partly due to the advent of Whole Language!

During the last decade Whole Language became one of the instant watchwords supplanted into the educational jargon of the day. In effect, this program pitted freedom of expression, growth in a positive self image and the development of creativity in writing against the age old tenets of spelling, handwriting and even reading! How was this accomplished you say?

In a growing movement that happily has died down somewhat teachers were told that children would only write if they were given complete freedom of expression to create whatever they wanted with little concern about letter formation, spelling, grammar or punctuation. We were cautioned to consider the fragile feelings of a child who experienced red correction marks on an original piece of writing. Papers were to be hung up with errors and praise and encouragement coupled with group mini lessons attempting to correct errors plus individual help were proposed as part of the basic program. Peer and teacher conferences along with group and individual editing and sharing rounds out the prescribed ideas of this program. The classics and popular library works are used to teach reading. It is thought that basal readers using a controlled vocabulary are not only boring to children, but provide a poor quality of story materials. Armed with all of this information, teachers by the thousands starting singing the praises of Whole Language! Many embraced the program entirely without careful thought as to the consequences.

Realistically speaking, I find many fallacies in the Whole Language program as outlined. First and foremost, the establishment and maintenance of a good self-image is such a developmentally complex goal, one that begins before birth. How can red correction marks on a paper damage a child's self worth if they are the result of the co-editing process guided by a caring and loving teacher? If children understand that everyone, professional or otherwise is equally involved in editing and that publishers in the real world necessarily require original pieces to be read and corrected before binding, it's only natural that they would want to follow suit! Secondly, the mini lessons that are taught in the first grade Whole Language program are not sufficient to produce writers who can edit effectively using the rules of English grammar and punctuation. Besides young children have not had the time to establish a working bank of spelling words to cull from and use effectively. Simply listing words frequently used in a so called "writing dictionary" does nothing to introduce, inspire and perfect the use of the wonderful tool that a dictionary really proves to be. Nor does this method provide the drill and practice necessary to begin to cement vocabulary and language patterns in the minds of young children.

Happily, Whole Language advocates are correct in dictating that children should be totally "immersed" in beautiful poetry, prose and other genre. However, these original works should be read and re-read by many adults rather than assuming that six year olds can be taught the intricacies of early reading using such advanced materials. This method can only lead to frustration with average and below average youngsters. The establishment of a controlled vocabulary and strong phonetic skills builds a solid reading foundation by using known words and family configurations that have been taught by rote in a multitude of exciting ways. Coupled with selecting a broad base of ancillary materials, such as Big Books and securing multiple copies of library books as well as anthologies and weekly newspapers, children have a better chance to develop a love of reading, which usually leads to attaining good language and writing patterns.

In reality, all of the pieces of the reading - writing connection fit perfectly when skills in phonics, handwriting, creative writing, spelling, reading, language and grammar are taught in a loving, non-judgmental environment by a caring and motivated teacher who bravely takes on the same writing tasks she or he presents to the children. If teachers are truly enamored with their career, they will see that all of these puzzle pieces can only fit together if the teacher is enthusiastic, hard working and wants them to fit.

Actually, a well-rounded language arts program should contain the positive aspects of Whole Language plus anything and everything else that works. Remember that there are as many learning needs, methods and styles as there are children in our classes! There aren't enough days in the year or time in each day to "submerge" children in the beautiful language that is their heritage. Sadly, there is still not enough attention paid to the development of even a marginal speaking vocabulary in children of all ages. The number of so-called precocious children appears to be dwindling as our society races toward goals involving power, glory, financial independence, and the liberation of women without any enlightened consideration given to the casualties incurred, namely an increase in violence, loneliness, physical and mental abuse, the often devastating media assault on our minds and the passive and immature language traits displayed by the children of today. There is little or no time to talk to anyone anymore, least of all children. Everyone is on a veritable merry-go-round of activities, some of which are totally "out of sink" with the fundamental needs of youngsters. How often do we hear the cry, "I don't know what to write about."?

The media in general and specifically television has become the instant baby-sitter of the eighties and the nineties. Gone are the days when imagination ruled and children were free to think, create and spread their wings in a non-threatening environment. Today even with all the brightly colored materials, educational tools and pre-schooling available, children are still sadly lacking in an expressive speaking vocabulary! This deficit seems to be wide-spread throughout the grades and high school as well.

Children talk in one word sentences which often prove to be just grunts or poorly enunciated speech patterns. They have little or no respect for the beauty of oral expression and worse, there are no models for young people to emulate. A rich vocabulary seems to be on the bottom of everyone's list or perhaps not even on the list. This is evident when PSAT and SAT testing time rolls around. The verbal section almost always appears to be more challenging and intimidating than the math reasoning section. The explanation could be that the teaching of math is more cut and dried and so the answer one comes up with is either right or wrong. There are no degrees of right in math. Vocabulary development is not something that one can cram for over a short period of time. The words of our language are so complex, filled with multiple meanings creating nuances that can influence comprehension in a very critical way. Intermediate, middle school and high school students don't read independently for fun anymore. Instead they opt for receptive, sedentary and passive entertainment provided by video games, movies, amusement parks and the like! This creates a devastating scenario for the cultivation of a love of reading and the development of a speaking vocabulary that can even loosely be termed as adequate!

All teachers teach reading vocabulary on all levels of instruction, but few educators are tuned into the systematic development of a viable speaking vocabulary. Just talk to five and six year olds and you will observe varying degrees of language ability. The same over-worked words are used repeatedly with few new additions planned and programmed in by the adults in a child's world. I therefore propose the creation of a separate strand of language arts instruction addressing this need. It would basically require the "immersion" of all students in a "creatively spiked barrel" of vocabulary words commensurate with their age and experiential levels taking into account the literature, social studies and science curriculum to be covered in a long range continuum. In addition, pre-school children would have to demonstrate a knowledge of the basic environmental vocabulary existing in our world, ie. names of animals and their young, words for furniture, clothing, tools, as well as plant names, toys, vehicles, household items, body parts, building materials, sports equipment, color names etc. Later on the vocabulary and dictionary assignments must not be simply a boring part of standard homework assignments as so often is the case, but rather exist as a living entity in daily discussions, critical readings and naturally all writing! We cannot hope to be recognized as a world power of educated citizenry, if our children cannot comprehend college level textbooks and demonstrate the ability to write a thoughtful, critical and well composed composition on a given topic. All high school seniors should be able to write an error-free expose on any topic. It is all too obvious to me that reading, spelling, grammar and speaking vocabulary development are subjects that are dying at a rapid rate in public schools all across our country.

It's shameful to discover that the U.S. is far out-distanced academically by countries like Germany, Japan, France and England. Our children spend less time in school and as a group they don't seem to view education as a top priority in their lives, even though our government appropriates huge and endless sums of money on all levels to cover one educational fad after another. In contrast, all too often the subliminal societal message of today promulgates the value of attaining a high degree of social awareness, the relentless pursuit of fun and the industrious acquisition of money at any cost.

In my view, all adults must make a concerted effort to raise significantly the educational standards of our country from the distant back woods areas to the major industrial cities and every place in between. We have to resurrect the basics in a core-centered curriculum method of instruction and include, emphasize and test handwriting, grammar, spelling, the study of geography and the memorization of addition, subtraction, multiplication and division facts as well as measurement conversions, time, length, dry and liquid measurements, money values and percents to name a few! All of the above are currently either lost subjects or in great jeopardy of becoming "dinosaurs"!

Year after year I have noticed how handwriting skills are dropping in importance. Have you ever tried to read a doctor's prescription? Are they all either purposely or accidentally illegible? At the other end of the spectrum, Nursery schools don't seem to attempt instruction or retraining in pencil or crayon grasp, probably because many toddlers have been allowed to hold writing tools any way they choose. With the advent of the computer, handwriting is almost becoming an unnecessary skill. Forms can be scanned into the computer, bills can be paid and every kind of program imaginable has been created so that soon the joy of coloring will be totally replaced by "clip art" and color printers! I wonder if the satisfaction gleaned by the ancient Chinese and Japanese writers who painstakingly created lettering that was nothing short of works of art can be compared to that which is instantly created on a computer! It seems that our world is just spinning too fast, so much so that everything must be reduced to the lowest common denominator. We are expecting ever-increasing speed, clarity and a high degree of cost efficiency!

Technology is also responsible for the almost total disappearance of any mental math at all. High school students are expected to supply and use calculators for class work in math. Gone are the days when students were taught to visualize the problem and seek an accurate solution without help from mechanical wizardry of any kind, not to mention fingers! These brain exercises are so beneficial to the conditioning of our "gray matter"! Thus our country is deluged with cash register clerks who can't make change even when the total amount to be returned appears boldly before them in black and white. Vegetable and fruit market clerks often can't compute the cost of two lemons at a price of five for one dollar. The neighborhood five and dime store, soda shop and bakery have long been replaced by strip shopping and malls that often rival small cities. Children cannot hop on their bikes and buy penny candy or a loaf of bread as I did. Because of the fear of kidnapping, the absence of sidewalks and the distance of stores, the urban and suburban children of today have been robbed of their independence and the chance to practice all kinds of mathematical skills. Today, children sit behind computers and they play so-called, "hand-eye coordination" games, they solve violent action figure combat problems and stare intently at "Game Boy"! Money has no meaning to the children of today. I fear that machines will take over all the brain work that used to be incidentally developed as part of childhood!

Lastly, we have the case of the average man on the street who when asked to name the last five presidents or to name three rivers in the U.S. or the capital of Mississippi slowly begin to retreat into a shy withdrawal type behavior which can only point to a severe lack of a meaningful education. When geography and history were combined years ago, they formed the subject that became known as social studies. The idea was basically a sound one. Logically speaking it would seem that to internalize the concepts inherent in the study of the French Revolution, one would need to know something of the geography of the area. However, what slowly happened was a gradual decline in the geographical elements in favor of the over-all historical facts and concepts to be learned. Too much information was then packaged into the various courses of study. Thus, insufficient time is given to each topic and slowly the fascinating study of the geography of our world is given almost no recognition at all. This is a terrible mistake, with lasting consequences. Besides so much geography can be taught in the primary grades where the interest is at peak level and there is a crying need for the infusion of viable curricula!

So Kristen, I leave you with some "food for thought" to be sure! As you ponder your role in the future of public education, consider the ideas expressed above and perhaps you'll see fit to stand with me and defend the rights of our children to be educated in the subjects that are facing probable annihilation by educators who are short-sighted and prefer opting for technology at the expense of developing brain power that is a never-ending source of energy, enlightenment and can with devoted effort, encouragement and enthusiasm lead to happiness and ultimate self-actualization! Never underestimate the power you have within you to positively affect the lives of the countless children you will meet! I challenge you to do more than teach! Educate!!!

Gratefully,
Pat

Chapter 12

March 8th

Dear Kristen,

It's March once again- a new season, another reason to rejoice in the mysteries of life we see before us each day! As the earth and all its developing greenery begin to take in the enveloping warm air, heralding the budding of flowers, the birthing of new life and the awakening of all creatures large and small, so too must we reaffirm our beliefs, re-evaluate our goals and look once again in depth at the young people we are charged to educate!

By now, many skills in every area have been presented. Some have been learned, others have been introduced with mastery envisioned at a later date and grade. Learning patterns have largely been addressed and relationships, though often fleeting at this age have been attempted with varying degrees of success. Overall, things are moving along smoothly for you and a routine has been firmly established, thereby creating a secure atmosphere with an air of tranquillity for the most part.

Into this environment let me interject some reoccurring ideas concerning the topic of discipline. Why now you say? With the advent of "spring fever" six year olds can become lackadaisical and it's possible for them as well as for adults to temporarily lose sight of what we're all here to achieve.

Roughly translated, the word discipline comes from disciple, or "one who spreads his master's teachings". We are the disciples who mold and perfect society's teachings through training. What are society's teachings? The basic idea is to develop good people who live as law abiding citizens and are gainfully employed while they enjoy the freedom to pursue their own individual dreams of happiness.

Superficially, the word discipline exudes a negative connotation. It often refers to the mastery of such early skills as toilet training, dressing, putting toys away and learning the many other orderly routines of life. Later on disciplinary issues often refer to inappropriate language, lying, destructive behaviors and other hurtful infractions involving feelings. These presuppose that children are developing a moral code and are gradually able to transfer feelings from one individual to another. In the early grades as well as the intermediate levels, children are still grappling with issues of fairness and effective peer communication. There are many times when I feel that dealing effectively with incidents involving the above must supersede in importance over any academic skill I could be attempting to teach! Therefore, I consciously try to weave social issues into many areas, touching as many academic skills as possible each day. It is a concerted effort that I feel pays off in the long run, for truly there is no way to separate the human element from any academic subject we teach. Feelings enter into everything. A simple math word problem involving two children buying toys at a store could easily lend itself to having a social overtone. Then too, so many incidents occur on a daily basis involving conflicts of one kind or another. How you handle these sends a powerful message to children! Taking time to mediate allows children to see problem solving techniques in action. Furthermore, your attention in a non-threateningly positive manner gives children confidence in your ability to make sound adult decisions. This is surely something you want them to emulate in their own lives. If you show partiality, you lose points with children. When this practice continues reoccurring over the year, you could lose the intuitive and sensitive child who craves your example in order to gain confidence. Besides all children need to know that you like them no matter what they have done. When children are practically involved in mediation and see you as a benevolent judge, the benefits are invaluable. Older children will often mete out harsh punishments for themselves rather than lose face in our eyes. Younger children basically want to do the right thing, but often lose themselves in the "heat" of the moment!

Another crucial idea leading toward effective positive discipline is the practice of setting up as many academic and social situations as possible where children come out winners! Now I don't mean purposefully losing at games so that youngsters gain confidence. Simply put I am suggesting that children should be adequately prepared for any new skills that are taught. Never go forward without taking a few steps backward. Assessing where you are requires looking back and noting from whence you've come! Taking a learning risk involves developing courage and a ready supply of confidence to be able to use known skills and apply them to the task at hand. Besides when an isolated skill is placed back into the continuum, an overall feeling of closure or completeness is created. The benefits of this technique are invaluable and can be used in any area with any age group including adults.

Once a pattern of effective problem solving along with fair and appropriate expectations of acceptable behaviors is established and observed on a daily basis, children can move along in academic skill areas with hopefully few disciplinary concerns. The child who is both skilled and socially adept has no reason to act out or cause disturbances unless the home variable has been designated as problematic. The latter could and often does spill over into the classroom and must be addressed.

Isolation is one technique, but I would use it only when all else fails or a youngster is in physical danger. Separation from one's peers is the ultimate embarrassment and the social damage can be not only lasting, but set up a pattern to be followed from that day forward. The negative reinforcement can only further escalate the condition. As educators we are charged to uncover the reasons why children behave the way they do. The shy and secretive child is most difficult, because he or she does not really trust. Loneliness and other forms of hidden child abuse could push a child to act in deviant ways.

I find that the extensive use of the positive makes learning easier for all children. In order for growth to take place, children must be alerted to the passage of time and the changes observed. So often you can point to the day that the "light dawned" for a particular child. What a wondrous occasion to celebrate! Statements like, "I remember when you couldn't start a story! Now you can do it independently!", send the message that you are aware and proud of the achievements a child is making. Nothing means more than your praise!

Also, peer pressure can be used effectively with some children. It's only natural to want to feel part of the group. We all want to be loved for who and what we are regardless of our age. It's often very hard to be different. Only the very determined child will stubbornly resist the powerful motivation to belong heart and soul to the group. Acceptance brings comfort, camaraderie and a rest from seemingly endless competition.

At the absolute highest level, our goal must be to guide each child to be self-disciplined, for that is one mark of maturity that lasts a lifetime and largely determines the happiness, success and degree of self-actualization one can achieve.

Now, how is this feat accomplished? It can only be attempted let alone achieved if you as an educator, can be courageous enough to realize that you stand before your class each day and like a mirror, you reflect everything you are and everything you stand for at that very moment. You are essentially, an open book with many pages, depicting your likes, dislikes, your values, your beliefs, your joys and sorrows, essentially the whole gamut of feelings deep within your unique personality. What a wonderful opportunity you have to express who you really are in the presence of young developing minds and hearts!

Effective discipline comes from consciously developing respect, fairness and love while living it in a seemingly unconscious or natural fashion. It must be felt in order to be mirrored for children to instinctively recognize and ultimately learn the concept. It must be valued by teachers and expressed through motivation, encouragement, praise and intense modeling each day.

It's another "tall order", you say! However, even at this tender age the self disciplined are already visible. Look for the mature youngster, who has tasted success and who is self- directed, shows leadership qualities, makes good use of time, questions new concepts, requests enrichment work, acts responsibly and learns because learning is a desire deep within. When you spot these children, always silently and sometimes loudly praise their efforts so that their example may be followed. Give these children helpful responsibilities that elevate them in a humble way, so that they learn to respect the efforts and the position of others. Enlist the aid of such children as buddies in other classes. These and other techniques reinforce the idea that you see, appreciate and commend the self disciplined youngster.

Meanwhile, take a risk with the less mature. Go out on a limb for the shy child by making him the star of your play. Send the sad or quiet child on a very important errand. Encourage the disorganized child to deliver a neighbor's homework. Ask the talker to be line leader. Make the secretive one be your special helper for a day. Do these and a thousand other things that will give these children reason to stretch and grow into the expectations you have for them! Wait patiently and steadfastly for growth without nagging, hurtful comparisons and other negative comments. Show them your love by an unexpected hug, a deserved hand shake, or just a ruffling of their hair. Make personal contact with each child every day and you will be on your way to effective discipline. For the disciple in us must communicate love or the underlying message will be lost!

You see, discipline is not meant to be negative. Positive heartfelt strokes do more to achieve self discipline and self actualization than anything else! If you want the proper message to be internalized, you must deliver it personally at precisely the right time for the right reason and in the correct dosage to each child each day. That's what we, the disciples are really called to do!!! Without discipline, effective learning cannot take place! Go with it now, Kristen and in the "spring" of your career, the multitudes will most assuredly follow you!

Proudly,
Pat

Chapter 13

March 20th

Dear Kristen,

Did you ever stop and wonder just what this thing we call "school" is? I have ! One definition in the dictionary states that a school is an institution of learning! This idea might presuppose that learning only takes place in school!

Sometimes I think that as teachers we feel we have the market cornered on learning! Well, nothing could be further from the truth. Let me illustrate. A few days ago I was in my neighborhood mini supermarket. I happened to spy a truly brilliant father wheeling his toddler around in a shopping cart. He stopped all along the route selecting vegetables, fruits, jars, cans etc. and as he held them up, this "blue collar" worker said the name of the item and talked with his little girl about each. I was overcome with joy and praised that man for taking an active role in his daughter's early education. This enlightened father was well on his way toward providing the kind of learning environment necessary for the development of solid language skills at a time when stimulation is essential. If children are not enrolled in pre-kindergarten programs, it is even more crucial for parents to take an active role in language development.

You see, children are naturally social, inquisitive and generally observant little people. When allowed and encouraged to live life to the fullest, the experiences one can amass are boundless and indelible. Parents are our first and best teachers. They know more about how we function than anyone else. They have assessed both our strengths and our weaknesses and they are most sensitive to our fragile personalities. The parent-child connection is a powerful one in that communication is achieved almost by osmosis. Therefore, a school that does not take full advantage of the powerful role that parents play whether positively or negatively in the lives of children is missing a golden opportunity to further and continually educate parents as to effective ways to stimulate, supplement and motivate youngsters throughout the formative years spent in school. Educators need to see parents as allies rather than opponents in order for cooperative learning on all fronts to take place!

Therefore, an ideal school of my choosing would invite and encourage parent participation on many levels and in distinct capacities. First, I would reorganize and rename the existing P. T. A. groups who basically serve as fund raisers and party planners. The replacement initials P. T. P. A. would stand for Parent Teacher Participation Association. Monthly meetings would by chaired by the principal, one yearly elected parent and one teacher. There would be no executive board, which seemingly serves only to give some parents more status, importance and power. Instead, all parents and teachers would have equal weight in the decision making process. Voting would depend solely on the parents and teachers in attendance at any one time. Topics under consideration would have less to do with money-making enterprises and more to do with issues that directly affect the education, safety and general welfare of the children attending the school. Parents would from time to time become guest speakers in all the classrooms and thus help to disseminate knowledge of the outside world in the areas of business, science, computers, health, the media, government, and careers to name a few. Parents would also be called to be guest readers in all the classrooms so that children would continually be immersed in literature and thus grow to love and respect reading as a viable lifetime activity experienced by all adults!

My ideal school would consist of a K-12 program housed in a multi-level building or group of structures connected by breezeways either in a city or suburban area, preferably near a hospital, university, old age home and a supermarket. All children would be accepted into the program regardless of race, creed, age, behavioral issues, financial status or academic prowess! Classrooms of from 15-20 children would be equipped with a large one-way window to enhance the observation and evaluation of both teachers and students. The cafeteria would only serve cold lunches, thereby eliminating the need for a whole segment of food service considerations. Naturally, poor children would receive free lunch and access to before and after school day care programs, along with extra help and homework instruction provided by the high school youngsters, all of whom would be required to perform various kinds of community service.

Bus transportation would only be provided for children living a mile or farther from the school. Older children would be paired with younger children according to geographical area and all walkers in groups of two to six would be trained over the summer in a "Walk Safety" Program conducted by a team of parents. Older children would learn responsibility. Younger children would benefit from the social contact of more mature students and all participating students would benefit from the increased physical activity. Practically speaking, a definite dress code or uniform would be necessary to reaffirm equality and aid in proper discipline.

The elementary program would encompass grades K-8. There would be no choice in courses. A back-to-basics core-type curriculum would emphasize developmental Reading, Grammar, English, Math, Handwriting, Creative Writing, History, Geography, Science, Vocabulary development and Foreign Languages. Art, Physical Education and Music instruction would also be provided. A well-stocked library and media center would provide the extra materials necessary to enhance the all-around education of the students. This center would be situated between the Upper(9-12)& Lower(K-8) Schools along with the cafeteria and a huge auditorium, all of which would permit and encourage shared usage. The school day would begin at 8:00 A. M. and would end at 4 P.M. with half an hour for lunch!

Children would be heterogeneously grouped in classes of no more than 20 children and they would remain with one teacher except for instruction in Art, Music and Physical Education. There would be no team teaching based on ability groupings on any grade level. Special education children would be totally mainstreamed and afforded modified curricula where indicated with services administered in each classroom by qualified teachers. Homework, study patterns and discipline would be stressed. Homework would begin in Kindergarten on an as needed basis, mostly verbal in nature.

First to third graders would have between one half hour and an hour of daily written homework. Grades 4 - 8 would be required to complete one to two hours of daily written and study homework. Report cards and conferences quarterly would create a climate of acceptance, cooperation and understanding resulting from an emphasis on communication that is accurate but also non-threatening! Seventh and eighth graders would begin community service programs on a small scale. Included in this area would be serving as a "buddy" for a younger child, reading to and playing with youngsters in the children's ward of the local hospital or assisting the early breakfast program etc. The frequency and type of service in grades 7 - 12 would increase with maturity, but would never exceed more than two hours per week on a rotating basis quarterly!

The High School program consisting of grades 9 - 12 would include all of the subjects mentioned above plus the after school mandatory community service which could be performed in nearby hospitals, old-age homes, and the before and after school programs, as stated above. Advanced students would have a curtailed High School program so that they could take advantage of the courses offered in the area university!

English and math High School courses would include the special preparation to take the PSAT and the SAT tests necessary for college admittance. Actually, the vocabulary necessary for the verbal and writing tests plus the ancillary skills in both areas would have systematically been presented in appropriate ways using high level materials, and frequent drills and usage beginning as early as the fifth grade! Creative writing would definitely be a daily activity on all levels!

High School classes of no more than 25 students would be set up in adjacent pods of four classes surrounding a lab room. Flexible scheduling without bells would be set up so that the students would circulate within the four rooms for two thirds of their day. The four teachers assigned to the pod would be responsible for the education of 100 students in the core subjects of Math, Science, History and Foreign

Language. The lab rooms would alternate between Math and Science use. The teachers would be required to know all 100 children and be accountable for their progress in the subjects taught. The pod teachers would meet before school to give extra help, discuss children, plan lessons cooperatively, meet with parents and evaluate the program's effectiveness. The last third of the day would be spent in the same pod area with the same four teachers all teaching English, Creative Writing, Vocabulary Development and Literature!

The High School day would begin at 7:30 A. M. and end at 4:30 P. M. with a half hour for lunch. There would be mandatory Music, Physical Education and Art classes on a rotating basis and all sporting events, team practices and work programs would be held after 4:30 and on Saturdays! A minimum of three hours of written and/or study assignments per night would comprise the homework standard, plus weekend projects or other assignments as necessary. Vacation and summer assignments would be a necessary requirement.

Trips using the facilities in the immediate area and involving the businesses nearby would help to enhance children's knowledge of careers and would assure the passing down of arts that can only be taught by masters. Sculpting, oil painting, cooking, architecture and masonry just to name a few are best taught on site. Special music programs and student concerts would be enjoyed by the entire school at once wherever possible.

Capable seniors in old age homes could become volunteer readers in the primary grades and clerical helpers in areas, such as the main office, library, etc., thereby adding a usefulness to their lives. All children could have the opportunity to entertain as well as learn from the segment of our population that is so often neglected, lonesome and "down" on life. These bearers of live history lessons that are unparalleled in scope, detail and realism could energize the curriculum in a very special way. The give and take occurring between the young and the old could spark endearing friendships besides tapping into a wellspring of experiences that would enrich the education of future generations!

Attempting to bring the world into the classroom is an important goal in planning any educational program. It seems to me that supermarkets are incredible ready - made classrooms in that they have all the materials necessary to bring math, nutrition and science alive. The myriad of lessons that could take place in a supermarket boggles my mind. What better setting to deal with money, plan a menu, price it and uncover the secrets of growing, harvesting, and preparing the bounty of fruits and vegetables on display in all supermarkets. Think of the speaking vocabulary that can be introduced, reviewed and worked into all areas of the curriculum because of frequent visits to the neighborhood grocery store. Skills in categorization, discussions of the four food groups, plus the packaging of foods, health and safety issues and tracing the path of foods from farm to market are all viable topics on hand. Such stores are a wellspring of information, there for the taking!

Hopefully by now you can see that my ideal school would take advantage of every opportunity within the area that could possibly be used to broaden the education of children. Then to, people of all ages and occupations would be used to provide the kind of realistic experiences that would remain forever etched in the minds of children. An underlying feeling of total cooperation in the community would have to be established, so that each adult realizes that he or she plays an integral part in the education of all the children.

The school community must function as a family unit with pride being stressed, encouraged and shown by example. The education of children would be the top priority in the community. As a result, I feel that juvenile delinquency in the form of drug and alcohol abuse, plus teen pregnancies and other anti-social behavior would decline. In the adult community the focus would be to emphasize that everyone is charged with the responsibility of protecting and preserving the talents, skills and arts that should be passed down from generation to generation!

Naturally the teachers employed in such a school would have to be well educated in all the core curriculum studies. They would have to demonstrate a mastery of the English language, both written and spoken. They would have to be charismatic teachers equipped to communicate their subject matter creatively, accurately and in depth, while projecting an inner joy which comes from a love of teaching children. A faculty of this kind would be charged with planning creative ways for the ideals and goals of the school to be met. There would be no time or space for personal adult egos to be fed and nourished. Rather a spirit of cooperation would have to be maintained at all costs.

The core textbooks and supplementary materials would be chosen by the principal and representative faculty and parent members. The infusion of appropriate values relating to humanity, cooperative living, caring for all life and property, respect and pride would be interwoven in all pertinent curriculum areas. Children would be taught manners, neatness and responsibility. They would learn to manage time effectively and enjoy cooperative relationships on many levels. Over time children would have to become attitudinally and academically secure in the realization that they are ultimately in charge of their own education!

Thus it is that in my view an ideal school should be run by administrators and teachers who would incorporate the value of learning for learning's sake in an atmosphere saturated with a multitude of experiences created to stimulate, challenge, enrich and fulfill all children. By teaching to the top of the class, returning to basic core curriculum studies, expecting the best from all children, and promoting stable work habits, we set the stage for positive goal oriented thinking. Thus, through the attainment of countless successes from little on, together with constant praise and encouragement, children would be highly motivated to pursue a college degree and a worthwhile career of their choosing.

You see, a school is merely a structure we send children to each day. If that building is not filled with meaningful experiences served up by adults who by their very example can communicate the value of learning, then we have failed miserably to educate our youth. Schools need to be viable structures that ooze learning in every form and forum. Then and only then will we as a nation be able to at least keep pace with the other world powers!

It is therefore to this end that I daily strive to inject the above goals and energy into my classroom, hoping that the small pockets of real education that children slip into will someday be magnified to include all children growing, learning and achieving in all schools throughout our great country!

A lofty goal you might say! Well, if we can think it, then we can do it!!!

Hopefully,
Pat

Chapter 14

April 26th

Dear Kristen,

It's Passover vacation, the perfect time to think about the joys and often the plight of "Parenting" as it exists in reality for us today! I know you've already been hit with the disturbingly rude and illogical parent who loudly proclaims, " Well, you're not a mother, so how would you know?"! In an effort to cover up her own guilt and inadequacies the said parent unloads her frustration on you, the teacher. It's as if understanding and warmth is reserved only for the female who has paid her dues in the delivery room! Well guess what? You've been unofficially welcomed to the 90's!

It wasn't always that way. In the 60's when I started, teachers were revered and elevated to an almost godly position. Even as a twenty-one year old fledgling I felt respected, honored and adored by children and parents alike. It was a different time. Few mothers were employed outside the home. The standard of living was much lower and many people truly believed in and cherished their values. I always felt appreciated and supported despite my young age and lack of experience, not only in teaching but mothering as well!

In those days a teacher's word was gospel and children were not over indulged, fresh or demanding. There were problems to be sure, but the effects of affluence was not one of them. More often the ills of poverty were responsible for the visible neglect and lack of academic achievement. Seasonal farm workers still made up a substantial part of the transient population in some areas. Few children by today's standards were found to have attended Nursery School or summer camp. Exotic vacations were the exception, not the rule. Family movies were just that, mostly Disney productions and weekly television sitcoms for children were delightful entertainment filled with positively uplifting stories filled with morals that gave children good vibes to guide their lives. Children were not fashion conscious at a young age and their activities were appropriate to their maturity and skill level. Everyone was satisfied with less. There was time for families to be families. Parents took their roles very seriously, because that was a major role they valued.

Extended families were more popular then and children often benefited from grand-parenting on a regular basis. School was one of the focal points of life. Participation in school events was looked on as crucial and school spirit was to be maintained by everyone's efforts. There was less competition among parents and more mature developmental goal seeking. In short, cooperation was the means to attain a good education for all children!

However, the winds soon changed. With the advent of Disney World, the cabbage patch doll, the explosion of technical advances in the media, a large degree of prosperity and the decline of real religious fervor, many parents have almost " taken leave of their senses". They have confused the wants and needs of their children, under the guise of giving this generation what they themselves missed! In some cases the damage has been irreparable! Children who came into this world with innately strong gifts made nothing of their talents. The values of today are often so superficial as to be downright disgusting! Material wealth and the acquisition thereof occupies too prominent a position in the minds and hearts of many, children included! The joy of work is gone and even the slightest favor often comes with a hidden price tag. The subliminal or overt lessons that are regularly taught, broadcast and praised are ones that stunt the growth of self discipline and rarely lead to any real happiness!

You are a product of this generation, but you are one of the lucky ones. You have parents who had the insight to realize that you needed to find and follow your own path in an atmosphere of acceptance and love. They knew that an excess of material goods would not develop your character or help you discover or reach fulfilling goals. The experiences you had as a child were appropriate and helped you become independent as you searched for your true self within realistic limits. You learned the value of close family relationships and this has created an inner happiness and peace within you that was apparent to me right from the start! The dedication and convictions you display are directly related to your family's values.

Kristen, you chose your career wisely and you are filled with the excitement of the challenges ahead of you. It's been a difficult year thus far, but you have passed each of your tests with flying colors! You have been faced with nearly every problem one teacher could possibly experience and you have determinedly

NOT knuckled under! You are a winner!

Remember that the pressures on parents today are enormous! They are constantly involved in "keeping up with the Jones's"! Some are decidedly misplaced geographically, while others have found themselves thrust into the role of parents with little or no background in the subject. Do you realize that parenthood is one of the few careers other than modeling that don't require schooling or a diploma? There is no real entrance age and it seems that more twelve year olds as well as more seniors are becoming first time parents. Hospitals don't hand out "How to" books for new parents and children are probably the only acquisitions in life that come without money back guarantees!

Being a parent must be a real ego trip! One day this cute little "bundle of joy" appears that soon walks, talks and begins to take on many of the parent's characteristics. When the parent observes and approves of the child growing up in his or her own image and likeness, all generally goes well. However, when a parent thinks, feels or expresses real and deep disapproval of a youngster over time, the damage is usually irreparable. Happily, most parents honestly love and deeply care about their children. They really do the best that they can to insure the proper growth and development of each of their children. Sadly, the number of child abuse cases is increasing, but that could partly be due to the emphasis that is currently being brought to bear on this issue.

With all this in mind, try to understand the frustration of a parent who daily lives with a child's acting out behavior or the embarrassment of a parent when he discovers that his youngster just doesn't measure up to the "normal" child and may require specialized instruction.

Even the parent who is decidedly on a mission to procure all the services the district offers is to be understood. Perhaps the parent is screaming for attention due to his or her frustrations with a different or difficult child. Don't we all shop for perfect products? Well, parents generally expect that children will be born problem-free.

Bad news is even more difficult to bear when it's your own flesh and blood! Sometimes even the prospect of obtaining prescription glasses for a child can be upsetting for the parent of today. What does this mean to a child's social well being? With the emphasis on college acceptance looming in the not to distant future for most children, I remember the father who told me years ago that his son was already accepted at his alma mater. I worried if the son could handle the pressure of an ivy league school, when his performance at the time was barely in the average range. Undaunted, the father unknowingly set the stage for possible failure in the mind of a youngster who was barely six years old!

Remember too, education is the only institution publicly funded that allows for open visitation. Utilities, local governments and the like rarely promote observation sessions. They operate in somewhat of a vacuum, caring not whether we approve of their procedures, personnel or billing practices. It takes an outcry of monumental proportions orchestrated over many years to elicit any kind of change in the giants of industry or government. Our individual powers account for minimal progress. Stifled in this way, some people take out their frustrations on teachers, using the payment of taxes as their right to complain and sometimes act out in emotional episodes. While most educators see this as an annoying interference, I view it as one of the checks and balances in place to keep us "on our toes" at all times.

Over the years it has become apparent to me that the degree to which we all parent the children of today is a vital variable that somehow has been lost amid all the other probable causes for the demise of public education.

Therefore, four years ago I started with a small group of concerned, vocal and supportive parents to meet monthly and provide a forum in which to discuss issues involving parenting. The topics ranged from discipline, respect, fears, sibling rivalry, routines, modeling, work habits, the teen years, grandparents, money, etc. and the core group carried over each year, as others joined. I felt that general discussions gave rise to individual problems and questions, which could be answered best by the parents with older children. There was safety in numbers and I tried to create a non-threatening environment within which everyone could function. It has given me great pleasure to know that positive ideas were reinforced as well as support shown for "tough love" theories.

I continue to feel that most parents operate within a vacuum and are often dreadfully alone with the problems they face. Hearing others speak often gives a parent the courage to try something else, knowing that it worked for someone. Just realizing that others have more difficult problems is also consoling. Then to, knowing that one's situation is not so very different from the norm softens the agony of a seemingly complex problem. My core group of three parents "flies up" in June, as their youngest children graduate from elementary school. Their problems could multiply, but with hard work, understanding and the benefit of experiences with older children in these families, I predict that if nothing else, these parents will be ever mindful of the importance of maintaining open lines of communication with their pre-teens. This will give them the edge they will need to set these youngsters on a successful path in life!

Remember, some day you too might be privileged to become a parent. It is an awesome responsibility that brings both joys and sorrows, though sometimes not in equal measure. Think about the values you were taught and the reasons why you were able to succeed, while others around you possibly failed. The answers to these and other crucial questions will help you to become the kind of parent your parents still are today!

As a teacher you are always the absentee parent and as such you must react to and decide in favor of a child's best interests. With all the different mores, customs, values and the like represented today, this becomes an enormous task. However, we must do it and we do it daily, whether we realize it or not. You see, each of us is a parent, for to teach is to be the part-time parent of many. Teach them well, Kristen! These children are our future and the possible parents of many generations to come!

Hopefully,
Pat

Chapter 15

May 14th

Dear Kristen,

The end of the year is fast approaching! As we begin thinking of our final report to parents, let us consider the educational and emotional climate we find ourselves in at the present. All across our country there is talk of vouchers, standards, portfolios, even accountability in the form of report cards for districts and individual schools. The academic pendulum continues to swing back and forth from one program to another creating an insecurity and an uneasiness among parents and some educators. What does this all mean? How do we fit into the BIG picture?

Since the advent of "free" public education for all children, schools and teachers have been under a veritable microscope. Although schooling for all is billed as "free", you are well aware that education is a costly business! In suburban areas, school systems are vast enterprises administered to by school boards comprised of residents who in most cases have little knowledge as to the inner workings of academia! You can be sure that the medical watchdog committee governing physicians, the A .M .A. is comprised of doctors!

Schools, therefore require funding which is collected in the form of taxes. Other than one's mortgage, the school tax bill is the most dreaded and largest compulsory expenditure all citizens most dole out on a regular basis. Seniors, singles and couples without children resent having to pay school taxes for children they don't have. Apartment dwellers often think they have escaped the tax because they are not homeowners, however everyone who resides in a permanent structure is billed according to a very exact set of formulas. When it comes to heat, lighting and telephone bills, residents at least feel that a service is rendered. Unfortunately, an often majority of people feel that voting down the school budget is the only way to express their dissatisfaction with the existing program.

Realistically, each community is charged with the education of the children residing therein. That is the philosophy of public education as it was originally set up. Naturally, citizens want to feel and see positive evidence that their money is being well spent. Therefore, it is disheartening to hear that there is still reoccurring debates over, "Why Johnny Can't Read?". You see there are too many High School students who can't read, write or compute accurately on even an eighth grade level. So-called College graduates often can't adequately fill out a job application. Many High School graduates can't write an error-free composition that has any style or depth. Also parents must provide costly instruction in vocabulary development and math review as part of the PSAT and SAT test preparations currently necessary for college acceptance. Sadly too many young people working in menial jobs in stores have difficulty computing or making change even when the amount appears in black and white on the register! Situations like these and others anger and frustrate the great majority of citizenry who are average hard working people, struggling on a daily basis to make ends meet. They wonder why twelve years of schooling often yields students who are poorly prepared by comparison to their European and Asian counterparts.

There is no question that the child of today is vastly different from the child of fifty years ago. The technological advances in all areas, the women's movement, single parent families, and laissez-faire parenting has in some cases robbed children of their childhood's, forcing them to grow up faster than they should, while in other cases allowing children to remain forever dependent due to an overindulgence in material wealth coupled with poor or no disciplinary guidelines!

However, the substantial public outcry for educational reforms necessitates giving real thought to weighing the financial aspects, and the constant bandying back and forth from program to program with the more likely culprit in the case of school reform being the quality and expertise of the teaching staff charged with educating our children!

Consider the mentality of a profession that protects all members once they become tenured!!! Whether the job is performed outstandingly or in a mundane fashion, year after year all teachers are placed on the same track and pay scale! It is realistically impossible to remove a teacher who is merely collecting a pay check without the benefit of an ironclad suit outlining documented testimony which could lead to conviction on a moral's charge! The frequency of "burn-out" is a major problem, especially considering the character of today's child. The latter is quick to convincingly threaten, even at the tender age of eight, to call a lawyer or even the abuse "hotline" when being disciplined. Double income family stress places an added burden on the teachers of today, either by their personal participation in this survival lifestyle or by the necessity of having to receive children affected by it.

If you add to all of the above the condition of college teacher preparation, it's no wonder that public education is so sadly in need of reform. Besides the "watered down" curriculum presented to young people on all levels from Kindergarten to college, graduates clutching their B.S .in Education generally have the watchwords, and the popular theories of the day, but often lack the motivation, the command of subject matter, the charisma, the dedication or the seemingly rare inborn ability to teach! The societal mentality is still one espousing the view that, "If all else fails, you can always TEACH!". Do you realize that it is infinitely much harder to win a title at a Miss America pageant, than it is to get a teaching degree? It truly seems that as a nation we are more concerned with the purchase and repair of our autos than the education of the next generation who may be doomed to enter the year 2,000 and find themselves "up a creek without a paddle"!!!

Presently, we are all involved with the upgrading of standards in the elementary and secondary schools including the addition of further testing in Reading, Math and Science every four years. This is all well and good if the basics are explored concretely, in depth and using the tried and true methods that really work. Unfortunately, the later have no glamorous name that would propel educators to "jump on the bandwagon" to pilot such programs and these methods also require an energy and dedication found only in pockets of education and in individual classrooms scattered throughout our country!

It seems a simplistic matter to resolve when you consider that in order to truly elevate teaching to the status of a recognized art, administrators must only make entrance into the profession much more than automatic and require a rigorous academic program steeped in the basic curriculum with emphasis on the acquisition of solid teacher skills and a totally revamped system of on the job training, otherwise known as student teaching!

The first basic problem on the college level is the widespread adherence to the notion and practice of beginning education courses in the junior year. In my estimation the education strand of a college education should run concurrently and parallel with the basic liberal arts studies required in the freshman and sophomore years. Therefore, entrance into the education department must occur on day one of one's college career. The acceptance of a prospective teacher candidate would depend on securing three letters of reference from various sources, excellent performance in a series of three interviews with different academic departments, achieving a high score on a 12th grade level Reading and similar Writing test besides evidence of at least a combined score of 1400 on the SAT ! These steps alone would serve to weed out probably two thirds of the candidates that heretofore would have automatically just waltzed into the program!

Secondly, teacher training would begin in the freshman year and would be in the form of classroom observation and mild participation for half day periods all year. The following program would be mandatory for all students regardless of licensing area requested.

Semester one would find a candidate placed in a variety of primary classes from 9 A.M. to 12 noon during the months of September and October. During November and December the same candidate would be observing and participating in intermediate classrooms from 9 A. M. to 12 P.M. respectively. In the second semester primary classroom observation and participation would take place from 12 noon to 3 P.M. during the months of February and March while intermediate visits would be scheduled from 12 noon to 3 P. M. in April and May. Meanwhile, the prospective candidate would be following a fairly usual liberal arts program along with at least two child development courses covering growth and changes in young children and adolescents. Students would be expected to take copious notes on classroom management, curriculum etc. and maintain diaries on at least two individual students in each semester! Written evaluations from the public school principal and elementary teachers involved with the candidate concerning dress, attendance, willingness to learn, relationship with children etc. must be of the highest order before continuance in the program is allowed. Naturally, the grades in the other course work undertaken must reflect above average achievement. Thus, after the freshman year students and college advisors would have a "good handle" on whether teaching could be a viable career for each candidate!

The sophomore year would highlight curriculum studies from Kindergarten through the 12th grade and would be mandatory for all prospective teachers no matter what grade, area or special area they hoped to pursue upon graduation! Increased participation for two to three whole days would be scheduled as such:

In semester one, September - December the student would visit one specific primary classroom only and be responsible for a written in depth study paper on one particular child. During semester two the candidate would spend two to three whole days in one specific intermediate classroom. There he or she would be required to plan a two to four week outline on a Science or Social Studies topic plus do an author study suitable for the intermediate class in question. The study would be presented in oral and written form to the college classmates and professor in charge of the course work for that semester. Again, written evaluations and acceptable liberal arts grades must go hand in hand with continuance in the teacher preparation program! By now various school districts and faculty members as well as college professors etc. would become intimately aware of the strengths and weaknesses of the prospective candidate. Perhaps the student might be leaning more toward the intermediate level as opposed to the primary school child and curriculum.

In the junior year of college one would begin the exercise of formal student teaching. Accepted candidates would be expected to be present every day, five days per week for the entire elementary school year. From September to December the student would be able to choose a primary class from Kindergarten to second grade. They would fulfill the requirements that are basically presently accepted, plus they must be evaluated by the public school personnel involved with the candidate. A written paper outlining and detailing the individual skills taught in every subject in the grade where the student teaching experience occurred would be expected upon completion of the semester. Other liberal arts courses would have to be taken either at night or in the summers between academic years. The second semester from February to May would be identical to the first except that the student would choose an intermediate class to study. All year long the students would share experiences and discuss curriculum skills in the follow-up college sessions. Again high grades must be achieved in all course work plus student teaching. By now each prospective teacher should have a very realistic view of what teaching in the elementary school is all about. Successful students at this point would begin preparing resumes for future reference!

In the senior year student teaching would continue to be comprised of a five day experience. The first semester experience from September - December would include placement in a middle school or junior high program where the candidate would be in touch with grades 6 - 8. This would help to round out the basic elementary school curriculum and child development factors that are crucial to working with this age group. Students would be expected to spend one month each working in a Math, English, Social Studies and Science class in either grades 6, 7 or 8. They would be expected to become familiar with the various courses and be able to order the skills from simplest to complex. An in-depth study of one student would also be required. Naturally, all other liberal arts courses would have to be taken in the evenings or in the summer. Written evaluations by school personnel would be placed in the college advisor's file for each prospective student. These reports would become the basis of a portfolio of information on all teacher candidates applying for licensing and permanent positions.

The second semester of the senior year would be somewhat different. Ideally by now all of the liberal arts courses should have been completed. Secondary students would be placed in a High School setting in the subject of their choice. If they were English majors, they would spend one month in 9th grade English, one month in 10th and so forth learning the skills, methods, techniques, materials and child development issues necessary to become adept at working with young people on those levels. Their course work would include in-depth studies of skill work, involvement in monitoring high school clubs, planning with teachers and other professionals and related seminars at the college level. Students would have to demonstrate proficiency in the subject area of concentration, writing plans and executing a four week theme project. As stated earlier, evaluations from all professionals involved, plus proficiency exams would be the basis for graduation and licensing!

For those seniors who plan to concentrate on the elementary or middle school programs, their final semester's task would involve choosing a grade or area of concentration that they hope to teach, and working with the children on that level in order to gain further expertise. High grades on the same proficiency exams as stated above plus suitable written evaluations would be pre-requisite for graduation and future licensing! Candidates interested in special education, reading, or counseling would be required to take a master's level program before actual placement in a public school setting.

Beyond college the first year of actual unassisted teaching experience for K-5 licenses should require a one year placement in Grade One, where a mentor with 10 - 15 years of experience further guides and advises the new teacher. Monthly sessions with a "Mentoring Committee" made up of three to five retirees, representing various levels of expertise would be held to acquaint the first year teacher with socialization and assimilation techniques that are largely overlooked in college courses. Issues of "fitting in" and knowing when to speak up and whom to consult are crucial to the success of a new teacher. Monetarily, full pay and benefits would be accrued, but there would be no union backing. Formal re-hiring by the district would depend on the degree of dedication, skill and productivity as evaluated by the principal, mentor, two other faculty members and two parents. Five out of six evaluations must be excellent!

Secondary teachers would have to spend their first year teaching Grade Six with exactly the same stipulations as for elementary licenses. Satisfactory completion of the entire program would enable candidates to be licensed to teach either K - 5 or 6 - 12! If a district hires a newly licensed candidate, that person would be on their own and begin the customary three year probationary period leading up to the granting of tenure!

As you can see the revision of the standards for entrance into the teacher training track is the key to weeding out people who are unwilling or unable to dedicate themselves to learn a very special craft. The proposed all-inclusive program places the responsibility for the education of our children squarely on the backs of teachers where it belongs. Therefore, it behooves all colleges and universities charged with teacher preparation to seriously review, revive, reform and renew their collective thinking on the part they directly and actively must play in the business of education for the year 2,000 and beyond. Otherwise, our country will be forever plagued with the more involved and burgeoning question, "Why can't Johnny read, write, spell, compute or live cooperatively within our complex society?"

"I rest my case" and leave it in the hands of those who will come after me, confident that America will one day come to its senses!

Assuredly,
Pat

Chapter 16

June 25th

Dear Kristen,

It's here once again, just as I told you it would be — The Last Day of School! It's as inevitable as night and day, the changing of the seasons, birth, death and taxes!

It seems like only yesterday that I welcomed you to our profession, our school and especially First Grade! Somehow ten months have come and gone almost in the "blink of an eye"!

I've watched you grow in so many ways as you felt your way through the myriad of "red tape", philosophies, programs, psychologies, presentations, occurrences, and disputes that are part of a typical school year. I've tried to listen to the laments you encountered, the questions you raised, the concerns you expressed, the opinions you've challenged and the decisions you have bravely stood by. I've marveled at your maturity, your courage, your dedication and the love you obviously have given to the children placed under your care. I've enjoyed all of our talks and even the tears we shed in the name of educating those wonderful five, six and seven year olds we've come to know and love!

I have started to come to grips with the thought that one day I, too will have to leave our wonderful profession. Getting to know you has restored my faith in the future of public education. Teachers like you are destined to face many new and challenging experiences in the next century. I am relieved to know that there are other bright and shining stars like you on the horizon. That will make leaving a slight bit easier for me, when that time comes. At least I now feel I can leave my original work, thoughts and ideas in deserving , loving and capable hands!

Yes, we've come to the end of the year! Ten short months have yielded much for many! Our little "students" have become just that! Those little "globs of clay" have lovingly taken on personalities, learning styles, various skills and they have confidently learned subject matter, made friends and have become somewhat adept in operating in the world of adults who control the realm of school!

In ten short months, most children have become one numerical year older and hopefully emotionally, psychologically and socially wiser. Each of the youngsters have begun the lifelong process of learning to read and communicate our wondrous language through the spoken and written word. They have been introduced to body language and communicating through facial expressions. They have developed a math sense and a social awareness. We have tried to broaden their horizons through the many experiences presented on a daily basis. We have emphasized strengths and worked on weaknesses. We've taught routines, work habits, and playing fairly. We built self confidence and a positive self image. We dried their tears, calmed their fears, protected, defended and loved them as we have attempted to turn each of them into skilled and independent students! We stayed late, came early, made countless phone calls, saw innumerable parents, scrubbed desks, cleaned messes, corrected work, assembled countless reports and attended endless meetings. We worked hours at home, stayed up late, came in sick, spent huge sums of our own money, lost many sleepless nights, and tried endless tricks to make learning both educational as well as fun!

We played games, orchestrated shows and displays, bandaged endless hurts, went on trips, fixed troublesome zippers, settled disputes, resurrected "smushed" lunches, searched for lost earrings, salvaged first teeth from the clutches of hungry garbage cans, buttoned countless art smocks, produced last minute homework and bus passes, timed medication to lessons, tracked down elusive siblings, celebrated birthdays, tied countless shoelaces, and hugged and cared for these children as our own. We reinforced moral behavior and universal beliefs. We fielded countless questions, sometimes in uncharted waters. We even ducked sneezes, "upchuck" and hacking coughs galore. We were "parents" in every sense of the word, until today!!!

It's the last day of school once again! I never seem to get used to the finality of it all. I still liken this experience to what a divorce must be like. Today is the day we must say "good-bye" to the children who have in many ways become our own. We've grown to love them for who and what they are. We rejoice in what they've become in such a short time. We appreciate the work they have produced and we forgive their mistakes, bouts of naughtiness and even their laziness or lack of motivation at times. We accept their humanness as we hope that they grow to become productive, happy and loving adults!

I always dread tearing apart the "family" concept

that I so lovingly have built upon since the first day! Never again will the exact group of children be assembled for the purposes of instruction. I begin my speech by thanking them for trying so hard to be all that I have expected them to be. I tell them that I appreciate all of their efforts and that I realize that in all cases the curriculum presented was difficult. I thank them for being so good and fun to teach. I tell them that I have learned so much from each of them and that I love and will miss them terribly! I caution them to do their very best in second grade. I tell them that listening , good work habits and excellent behavior are the watchwords for success in any grade. I tell them that all teachers teach the curriculum the best way they know how. I try to make them understand that they won't always love or even like their teachers. I reinforce the idea that they must never let go of their main task, that of obtaining the best education possible. I tell them that all teachers will not love them the way I do. However, they must still learn, knowing that I'll be there for them always. I'll still give free advice, fix hurt feelings, lend lunch money, smile and wave in the hall, and always have an endless supply of hugs ready for those in need!

If I ever make it through the above without tears, I'll know that it's time to leave teaching. What's the rest of the last day like? Well, the buses always seem to be early and as the children pack their report cards, autograph books and their last few simple belongings, I wonder just how I am going to get through the rest of this torturous day. I have the children line up and I look around at the boxes and the blank walls, and there I see a shell of a classroom, once alive with stimulating colors, activities and the results of all kinds of learning. Usually someone says or does something that really affects me emotionally and the tears of earlier begin anew. I wonder if my darkened sunglasses will save me once again. I doubt it!

As we enter the hall, I notice that the building is alive with anticipation and the pitch is at an all time high. I herd my children together in a last ditch attempt to keep them close to me. I dread rounding the corner and seeing the usual group of parents waiting, knowing full well that someone is bound to stop me and wish me a great summer. That's all it would take. Magically I make it to the door and realize all too soon that I am probably one of the last classes out. Hugging each one desperately as they run to their respective buses, I silently pray for the strength to survive with my colleagues watching.

After what seems to be an eternity, I manage to get all the children on their buses. I want to run inside and cry, but I know that I can't. There are children waving from every window on each bus. Some of them are calling my name as well as other faculty members' names. How can I leave?

In a carefully orchestrated symphony, all of the teachers are positioned on the east wing of the bus platform, waving, yelling, smiling, jumping up and down accompanied by the blaring of bus horns. I cower in the background and wave and wish the whole thing was over. Afterwards, the faculty runs to the west wing platform where the ceremonial ending is repeated, amid a chorus of "Free at last"!

Totally exhausted I enter the building quickly not wishing to speak to anyone. I go to my "sanctuary" and marvel at the quiet while I let my mind wander over the experiences of the year now gone by. I slowly pack my belongings, turn off the lights and thank God for allowing me the opportunity with His help to once again orchestrate the many miracles I've been privileged to witness. I take one long last look at my favorite room while I lock the door on another successful year. I leave tearfully realizing how exhausted I feel, but rejoicing in a fulfillment like no other!

Today is your first "Last Day", Kristen! I am glad that your response to it was similar to mine. As I head for home unable to speak, lost in my thoughts and feelings, I think of all the good things that happened to me this wonderful year. I am grateful to have met such beautiful children and their families. I have been fulfilled each and every day and I pray that God will once again give me the strength to be all that I can be in order to make a difference in many new lives.

As I arrive home, I try to never look back but only ahead to the next challenge. Long ago I painfully learned that some of the children who seemingly adored me all year soon forget to say hello, or hold a door open, but instead acted as if they were temporarily blind while I struggled with a heavy load. However, there are those who come back years later and in effect say "thank you"! It's an evolutionary process that seemingly must take place in order for the successful roll over to be accomplished. To those very extra special few who remember and internalize what we have done, I am endlessly grateful. Undaunted we must continue to rise above our fears, our tears, our disappointments and frustrations, for come September a new group of shining, loving and adoring little faces will look up at us with all the wonder that five and six year olds possess and we must once again provide, create and orchestrate a new set of miracles!

Congratulations Kristen! Yes, You Are A Teacher!!!

Now and always,
Pat

CONCLUSION

As we all head at breakneck speed toward the 21st century, let us be acutely aware and mindful of the task before us. History is replete with the recorded instances of the failure of educational programs to "hit the mark"! The ever-present pendulum seems to be always ready to excite and incite everyone to jump on for the ride!

Schools are the institution through which our children pass as if on a conveyor belt or amusement park ride. During those twelve academic years and beyond, they are bombarded with a plethora of supposedly stimulating experiences served up by a variety of adults each of whom adds skills hopefully but also varying philosophies and attitudes just by their sheer example. Sadly, there is painfully little time to accomplish the educational task at hand. In reality, the standard six hour teaching day is reduced to probably four and a half hours of prime teaching time when you factor in lunch, special subjects, passing time, interruptions, and the notorious practice of fragmenting instruction.

While we educators and parents alike speed youngsters along their appointed tracks, they often fall victim to the many pitfalls in their path, over which they have no control. Each child is part of an unwittingly captive audience, totally dependent on the wisdom and expertise of all the adults in his or her environment. The organizational and planning skills, plus the ability to parent and discipline in an enlightened fashion, not to mention the acquisition of skills and knowledge all directly contribute to the end result.

As a sophisticated society we must be ever cognizant of the absolute necessity of passing the "torch" to the next generation. In so doing, it is crucial that all adults make the education of all of our children the prime concern in our nation. This is not accomplished simply either by approving vast expenditures of money for materials or investing in every educational theory or whim that comes "over the pike"! What is needed is a complete restructuring of the curriculum and standards from pre-school through college as well as the philosophical organization of schools and the methods of hiring teachers. When and if this is accomplished, the teaching profession will be elevated to the stature it so richly deserves! The end result will be a school system which actually educates youngsters and adequately prepares them to become fulfilled, independent adults ready, willing and able to take their place in and contribute to the ever-changing society at large!

You see "schooling" must be portrayed as a valued privilege rather than a given! It must also be viewed by youngsters as a participation rather than a spectator "sport"! Too often the teens of today appear to waltz through school as if they are in a "holding pattern" till reaching full citizenship at eighteen years of age. Devoid of values, skills, or goals and consumed by the violence, vices, vegetative behaviors and the barrage of media stimulation, the children of today are doomed to enter the welfare system of tomorrow rather than assume significant national, state and local leadership roles.

Thus we are all charged with creating an environment for children right from birth that teaches, encourages, and models the value of learning for the sake of learning. Schools are only structures or institutions but we must continually find ways to infuse life and love into those four-walled edifices, and diminish the over-abundance of "red tape" so that the miracles of discovery can occur. Parents and teachers alike must systematically envision, create and promote the idea of schooling as being a lifetime process with no end! Unlike the amusement ride that finally comes to a standstill to either the relief or dismay of the child, acquiring creative thinking skills and problem-solving techniques will always be learned abilities that will forever be the distinguishing mark of the educated in our world!

We do not have the luxury to overlook the education of any child, for it is the right of every person born in this world to be given the tools with which to achieve peace, success, happiness and fulfillment! Schools are the established vehicles charged with this task. If public education and the advance programs in college provided to complete the cycle are not revamped, it would not be impossible or unreasonable to assume that some other organization or institution could rise up and assume this crucial societal responsibility!

"Give me a fish and I'll eat for a day. Teach me to fish and I'll eat for a lifetime"! In an effort to help accomplish this goal, I have joyfully and lovingly written this work!

ABOUT THE AUTHOR

Let me introduce myself. I am "Thursday's child"! I began as a "pre-baby boomer" born during a particularly bad weather period in the late fall of 1943. I was the totally wanted and adored first child of Doris, born in Munich, Germany and John, a native New Yorker of Swiss, English and Irish descent. I made my appearance at a time when nearly everything was rationed and the flu temporarily felled so many people that I was ten days old before I met my father!

My parents, my most important teachers were average people who lived a modest life, believed in God and cared for their fellow man. I was given all the necessities of life and few of the luxuries. Rather I wallowed in the love and adoration my parents showered on me. Religious and societal values were the core of my upbringing. Happily though, I was given permission to be a child and to slowly discover and learn through guidance, encouragement and selfless parental devotion all the skills that even now serve me in good stead as an adult!

Mine was an idealistic childhood even after the birth of John Jr. in 1951! Although this so called "bundle of joy" was not the sister of my dreams, his birth proved to be monumental in that it and he changed my life forever. John was different right from the start. His poor vision foreshadowed more severe problems perhaps stemming from the light case of German measles my mother detected during her third month of pregnancy. This wiry, highly active and obviously bright boy resisted training, discipline and proved to be more than a mild annoyance to many of his teachers. By age seven John had been diagnosed with a brain tumor, and the operation for removal of same had been billed as highly risky. Needless to say, my "sweet sixteen" birthday was spent in New York Hospital praying for the successful conclusion to a nightmare of an operation on the little brother who charmed his way into my heart and my life!

The next two months added the kind of stress many families crumble under. Somehow we all pulled together and accepted the inoperable but benign brain tumor as the inescapable fate we were dealt!

Teaching and living with a low vision child, who was termed legally blind along with accompanying physical restrictions is a "tall order". Learning to read, write and compute became a painstakingly difficult process that could literally consume a family. I know it did ours!!!

John seemed to bring out the best or the worst in both the adults and classmates placed in his various learning environments. During the resulting elementary years I was horrified to meet mediocre as well as inhumane adults who called themselves educators. Sadly, no outstanding teachers surfaced to rescue our "different" child! It was during my high school years that I probably decided for sure that I wanted to teach. All those years of playing school in the cellar, which were some of the most fulfilling experiences for me proved to be the precursor of a bright future.

I went on to complete my elementary teaching program of studies at Hofstra College while finding time to help John begin his grueling four year high school program which would take five years to master. It was a regimented life with little time for many of the social and other experiences young people of our ages enjoyed. Our family was on a mission to educate John despite the very little help obtained from a school system existing in a functionally pre-special education era!

The lessons I learned being the older sister and amateur teacher to John proved to be the experiences that helped form my unshakable ideas and opinions on the appropriate methods, materials, philosophy, and psychology to be used as a teacher of young children. I helped plan, organize and create the tools that proved to realize our objectives. The many hours of reading, outlining, studying, tape recording and drilling slowly became part of my life. John and his unusually severe handicap was an accident of life that placed me on an early and easily identifiable course and it is a path of fate that I have never regretted taking!

Other tragedies further complicated our lives over the years since I proudly accepted my first teaching position upon graduation in 1965! The three year illness and subsequent death of my father in 1968 created a myriad of problems, emotionally, financially and academically. I was thrown into the "head of the household" position at the age of 24! Faced with providing a college education for John and supplementing the meager income left to us by my father, Mom was forced to seek employment at the age of 52! Through it all we stuck together and made life work!

Over the following thirty years John amassed many skills. He painstakingly built a stereo system from scratch, developed a love of music and swimming and even attempted with help, ice skating, cross-country skiing, dancing and basketball. Currently he is a clerk at a community college and has become an outgoing participant in life who is loved by all!

I can't believe that I have just completed my 32nd year of teaching with all but the first year having been as a first grade teacher. My experiences in that capacity have included serving as building grade chairman in the seventies, helping to pilot a non-graded interage primary family and developing an individualized reading continuum. I was honored with the esteemed P. T. A. Life Membership award in 1972 and recommended by my principal to be included in the 1975 volume of the "Outstanding Elementary Teachers of America"! Lately, I have been studying the development of vocabulary in grades K - 12 as well as implementing and conducting a monthly Parenting Program since 1993. Last year I initiated a multi-age workshop for children with special needs, which will continue to meet on a monthly basis. Probably my most prestigious honor to date would be that of a former student who nominated me to be included in the 1996 edition of "Who's Who Among America's Teachers!

I truly love my career more now than when I began! My family and I went on to face the complications of four major surgeries undergone by my Mother who has always been a tower of strength and the main "supporting beam" of our family! The love she instilled in us has been the underlying basis of our successes and at 81 she continues to be a dynamic force in our lives! With all that we've experienced, I continue to enjoy writing, reading, photography, gardening, skiing, skating, basketball and extensive traveling!

As I look back, I never regret passing up "the road not taken" ! Through the selfless dedication of my outstanding parents and the intense brotherhood that grew out of a "twist of fate", I am a fulfilled adult who grows to love life, writing and teaching more each day!

Yes, I am "Thursday's child" and I have "far to go"!!!

Patricia Donat
August 30, 1997

HELPFUL HINTS

1. Keep lessons short 15-20min.(Fall only).
2. Follow a noisy activity with a quiet one and keep alternating.
3. Change location of lessons within the classroom.
4. Try to call on children who are shy only if you are fairly sure they have a right answer. This builds confidence.
5. Change seating within an arrangement for positive reasons that are known to all.
6. Change the seating arrangement at least every marking period. It's time to make new friends.
7. Keep shy, disruptive or needy children as near as possible to where you spend the most time.
8. Circulate around the room during follow up drill or whole group instruction to check on listening skills and mastery.
9. Find a thousand ways to praise each child every day.
10. Be sure that evidence of written work is displayed for each child.
11. A late lunch could suggest a morning snack and visa versa.
12. Allow about 5 minutes to walk to lunch or special subject classes depending on distance.
13. Preparing for art class requires about 10 minutes. (put on smocks).

14. Train children to fold smocks and store neatly in a box or other container.
15. Never allow more than 5 children at a time to do any one thing, ie. water fountain drinks, getting coats, lunches or extra bathroom visits.
16. Monitor closely unpacking and packing up, line formation, walking in the hall, fire drill behavior, bus departure etc.
17. Be at the door every morning to greet the children with a smile and a word of praise.
18. Say good-bye to each child individually as they board their respective buses.
19. Choose line leaders, helpers, attendance takers and errand runners fairly and equally.
20. Check for neatness in closets on a daily basis.
21. Try to catch each child each day doing something great so that others can emulate the desired behavior.
22. Give one sentence directions, ask someone to repeat what you said and then check to see if the direction was followed.
23. Set out all materials to be used the next day the night before.
24. Read a book or poem each day during snack time.
25. Save all the materials used each month in file folders for ready reference the following year.
26. Keep sample of first handwriting and creative writing assignment for comparison use throughout the year.
27. Take photos of children the first day and watch them grow over the year.
28. Computer labels are a great way to identify all of the children's workbooks, notebooks & folders.
29. Invite parents to write an essay about their child

covering the salient points you are interested to know early in order to help each child.

30. Review the learnings of the day plus the homework assignment at the end of the day so they are fresh in each child's mind.
31. Be sure that independent work is carefully explained and ordered so that monitoring become easier.
32. Visit the bathrooms as a group after snack and lunch to discourage disruption of whole class lessons.
33. Never allow recess at the very end of the day as that defeats the purpose of the break.
34. Discourage visits to the nurse unless you see blood, or you suspect fever, pink eye, sore throat or other legitimate problem.
35. Band-aids and water go a long way to cure anxiety - bearing first grade "illnesses".
36. Select a child who needs an emotional boost or special praise to go on a responsible errand.
37. Make parents feel welcome in the class by having them attend birthdays, give talks on their careers and assisting or directing creative projects.
38. Put on a culminating show of some kind to highlight all that has been learned that year.
39. Invite parents to Portfolio Day and make it a double barreled experience, that is: praise for the children's work as well as an opportunity to educate parents on the skill's progression.
40. Absence notes & bus passes should be kept in a large envelope & saved all year.
41. Attendance cards are a legal document and must be filled out in black or blue ink.
42. Placing a mark on the duplicate cards denoting the end of each marking period and recording the total

absences in pencil saves time when compiling report card info.

43. A pocket folder positioned near the door containing a class list on one side for fire drills and a handy bus list on the other side facilitates last minute queries.
44. An invitation sent to each child's home prior to the first day makes each child feel more secure and illustrates the importance of first grade.
45. Collect trip money in envelopes that parents clearly mark with name, trip, amount of money etc.
46. Keep trip money in the separate envelopes in a large business envelope with class grid sheet attached and names checked.
47. After trip is over it is easy to return money to absent children.
48. If dividing children in groups for a trip, it might be wise to have the child belonging to each adult present in that group. A list of names should be provided for each parent along with any special info, ie. maps, time schedule etc.
49. Bring comfortable shoes, an umbrella, a smock, a sweater etc. to store in your personal closet.
50. An autograph book with a personal and an individual entry written by the teacher is a wonderful ending activity.
51. A monthly class newspaper helps to keep parents abreast of what is going on the class.
52. Children must be dismissed by the office after a required signature is given.
53. Parental permission is required for all class trips and play dates to visit friends.
54. All absences require a note of explanation.
55. All occasion wrapping paper makes a great non-

fading covering for dull bulletin boards.

56. Take time to establish work habits and rules at the beginning and things will run smoothly for the remainder of the year.
57. Think about delaying written homework until preliminary writing on lines has been carefully introduced.
58. Make homework a privilege not a given!!!
59. Instill orderliness by checking "cubbies" or closets daily and praising neatness.
60. Photographs of the children in action either in groups or singly add so much to the vibrancy of a classroom.
61. A quarterly letter along with report cards and other pertinent academic info. keeps parents informed and makes them an integral part of the learning process.
62. Square old-fashioned plastic washtubs are great organizers for reading group materials. As each group is called, the materials are ready to use.
63. Keep a file or notebook of your favorite children's books and poems for ready reference.
64. Keep a notebook of spelling dictation sentences organized by phonetic or sight based categories.
65. All kinds, colors and shape erasers provide a useful and sought after prize for first graders with dynamite answers to tough questions.

CLASSROOM SUPPLY LIST

TOOLS:

- hammer
- screwdriver
- hand broom/dust pan
- hand shovel
- fly swatter

CLOTHING:

- sweater
- umbrella
- extra shoes
- old sneakers
- other female supplies
- aspirin etc.
- hard candy
- extra stockings
- make-up
- boots
- straight pins
- rain jacket
- smock/apron
- safety pins

OTHER:

- Band-aids
- napkins/paper towels

tissues
tissue wrapping paper
paper plates
plastic utensils
pot holders
ice cream scoopers
can & bottle openers
salt & sugar
paper cups, 5 & 7oz.
coffee mugs
thermos
cookies
cookie jars
pointer
yardstick
Fantastic
liquid soap dispenser
sponges(large & small)
Comet
plastic bags
silver foil
Saran wrap
brown paper lunch bags
sandwich bags with zip lock
playground ball
plastic bats & balls
bubbles
glitter
paper doilies
stickers
kite
whistle
dominoes
egg timer

apple corer
dice
book ends
dust rags
pail
sidewalk chalk
hooks
extension wire
bins and organizers in various sizes
flannel backed vinyl tablecloths
cooking pots
flower pots
one burner hot plate
twist ties
camera, film
birthday candles
gift wrap for bulletin boards
playing cards
addition & subtraction cards
rulers(inch & half inch)
chalkliner
kiddie scissors
fun-tac
pencil grippers
pocket folders
manilla folders
watercolor markers
permanent markers
large 24″x 36″ lined chart paper

COLLECTIONS:
buttons
ribbon
blocks

books
pipe cleaners
egg cartons
coffee cans
tennis ball cans
shoe boxes
yarn
magazines
newspapers
packing "noodles"
beads
string
play money
feathers
plastic colored clothespins
toilet paper rolls
paper towel rolls

MATH CURRICULUM
Grade 1

I. SET THEORY

A. Numeration

- Naming objects
- Identifying sets
- Categorizing sets
- Constructing sets (concrete objects)
- Ordering sets (size relationship, numerical relationship)
- Counting sets
- Empty set
- Comparing sets (=, ≠)
- Changing sets (adding to, taking from)
- One-to-one correspondence
- Equalities and inequalities (concrete objects)
- Greater than – less than signs
- Writing numerals 0-10
- Reading number words
- Comparing sets and numerals using objects, numerals and rods
- Abstracting notion of inequalities 8 > 7

B. Addition Operation

1. Sets

- Joining two sets (objects and pictures)
- Plus sign
- Symbols for missing quantities or operational signs
- Use of words, and; is

- Writing plus equations for picture problems
- Drawing plus equations using sets
- Writing equations for spoken stories
- Addend, addend, sum relationship
- Reversal – sum, addend, addend
- Horizontal and vertical addition
- Cummutative law of addition
- Adding 1 to a number; 2 etc.
- Algebraic solutions
- Patterns for sums to 10
- One missing addend (concrete objects, balance scale)
- Two missing addends
- Missing addend in equalities
  $1 + 3 = 2 + ?$

2. Number Line

- Points on a line; infinity (both ends)
- Drawing a number line
- Numbering a line
- Showing one quantity on a line
- Directional Movement
- Showing two or more quantities on a line
- Showing addition on the number line
- Solving equalities where sum is needed
- Writing equations for pictured jumps
- Solving equations where addend is missing, but jump is shown

C. Subtraction Operation

1. Basics

- Notion of diminishing sets
- Drawing subtraction operation sets
- Minus sign

- Writing & drawing equations
- Sum, addend, addend relationship
- Horizontal & vertical subtraction problems
- Writing equations for spoken stories
- Relationship between addition and subtraction
- Converting plus equation to minus
- Number families

D. Numeration-Place Value

- Number sequences to ten (before, after, between)
- Writing numerals in order
- Isolating groups of ten
- Numbers greater than ten
- Counting to 100
- Reading numerals to 100
- Writing numerals to 100
- Counting by tens
- Tens and ones concept
- Expanded notation

E. Fractions

- Recognition of shapes (square, circle, rectangle, etc.)
- Recognition of equal division of shapes
- Whole vs. parts
- Recognition of equal division of sets
- Whole vs. parts
- Recognition of fractional numerals, 1/2, 1/3, 1/4
- Read fraction words (one half, etc.)
- Meaning of numerator and denominator

- Division of shapes into halves, thirds and fourths
- Division of sets into same
- Solving equations i.e. 1/2 of 10 + ?

F. Multiplication

1. Number Line

- Equal intervals
- Drawing specified number of jumps and specified intervals
- Convert to times equation
- Write equation for pictured jumps
- Using sets in an array
- x sign
- Drawing pictures for x operation
- Convert to times equation
- Commutative law of multiplication
- Horizontal and vertical multiplication
- Relationship of addition to multiplication
- Counting by tens, twos, fives, threes, fours

G. Division

1. Basics

- Counting a set
- Finding groups of objects in a set (specified #)
- Verbalize number of groups in set
- Draw pictures for division operation
- ÷ sign
- Convert pictured problems to division equations
- Horizontal and vertical problems
- Relationship of multiplication to division

2. Number Line

- Total interval
- Recognize division into equal groups
- Verbalize result
- Commutative law of division
- Relationship of division to subtraction

H. Geometry

- Recognition of points, lines, angles, curves
- Draw points, lines, angles, curves
- Review all shapes
- Draw free hand shapes
- Draw lines of specified length
- Measure shapes of specified length
- Draw shapes of specified length using a ruler

I. Measurement

- Measuring tools
- Solid, liquid, linear measure
- Ruler, standard linear measurement
- Points on a ruler
- Inches, feet, yards
- Measure objects in room
- Draw figures of specified length
- Dozen, half dozen
- Cups, pints, quarts, gallons
- Conversions; inches to feet, quarts to gallons
- Purpose of measurements

J. Time

- Instruments used to measure time
- Numerals on clock face
- Hour and minute hands

- Interval of time between numerals
- Tell time by minutes and/or hours and minutes
- Use forms: 8:40, 7 o'clock, half past 6, twenty minutes before 9

K. Money

- Recognize penny, nickel, dime, quarter, half dollar
- Learn value of each coin
- Review counting by 5's & 10's
- Counting change
- Solving story problems

L. Miscellaneous & Enrichment

- Equalities and inequalities of type $4 + 3 < 1 + 9$
- 3 addend addition
- 2 and 3 place addition and subtraction
- Addition and multiplication tables
- Work problems – one and two step involving the four operations
- Solving for the operation
- Advanced place value: reading large numerals i.e. 34,198
- Graphs
- Roman Numerals
- Devising number systems
- Base arithmetic

II. CUISENAIRE RODS

A. Introductions

- Familiarization with rods
- Describe rods
- Discriminate between colors
- Establish similarity of same color
- Size comparison ("Show Me" game)

B. Skills – Readiness

- Staircase construction
- Reciting colors
- Difference between any two steps
- Memorization of colors in order
- Numerical keys: If white = 1
- Transfer to numerical values
- Interchange color and numerical value
- Proof of numerical value
- Greater than – less than using rods and signs

C. Addition Operation

- Construction of trains
- Measuring rods
- Verbalize train in colors
- Verbalize train equation in numerals
- Transfer addition of sets to addition with rods
- Commutative law of addition using rods
- Missing addend concept with rods
- Begin with sum; insert two addends

D. Subtraction Operation

- Introduce new operation as cover-up
- Interchange terms minus, take away, cover-up

- Show equation format
- Tell cover-up stories

E. **Numeration-Place Value**

- Review assigned numerical values
- Place rods in staircase order
- Consider possibility of adding to staircase
- Formation of numerals greater than 10
- Counting by tens
- Tens and ones concept
- Expanded notation

F. **Fractions**

- Change value of rods
- If red is 1, then.....

G. **Multiplication**

- Introduce new operation as cross (x)
- Show cross operation
- Write equations
- Cross, floor, train and equation are steps involved

H. **Division**

- Introduce quotient operation
- Use terminology (contained therein)
- Write equations

I. **Geometry**

- Use rods to form outlines of square, rectangle, etc.

J. **Measurement**

- Use various rods as unite of measurement

K. **Time**

- Use yellow rods to stand for five minute time intervals on clock
- Counting by fives

L. Money

- Use white, yellow and orange as coins
- Counting by ones, fives and tens

M. Miscellaneous

- Three car trains

LANGUAGE ARTS CURRICULUM
Grade 1

I. LISTENING

II. SPEAKING

III. READING

A. Phonics

1. Readiness Activities
   - Recognition of upper and lower case letters
   - Recognition of alphabet sounds
2. Sounds
   a. Short
   - Two letter phonograms ag, et, im, ob, un
   - Add initial consonants
   - Three letter phonograms ack, ell, int, ond, ulp
   - Add initial consonants
   - Add blends and digraphs

   b. Long
   - Three letter phonograms ade, eel, ipe, oan, ule
   - Add initial consonants
   - Add blends and diagraphs

B. Vocabulary

1. Sight Words
   - Levels A-E
   - Compounds
   - Synonyms
   - Syllables

- Antonyms
- Homonyms
- Root words
- Crossword puzzles

2. Incidental Vocabulary
   - Alpha big words
   - Subject area words
   - Individual high interest words

C. Language Forms

- s, ed, ing, ly, y endings
- s and es plurals
- 's (possessives)
- contractions
- variant plurals
- ful, ness

D. Comprehension

- Analogies
- Sequence of ideas
- Fact
- Inference
- Conclusions

IV. WRITING

A. Readiness

- Posture
- Pencil grasp
- Position of paper

B. Simple Skills

- Recognition of lines and spaces
- Position of dots above and below lines and/or spaces
- Forming dots, straight and slant lines
- Connecting dots

- Tracing shapes

C. Double Space Manuscript

- Writing name
- Formation of lower case letters
- Space between words
- Position of words in a sentence

D. Single Space Manuscript

- Isolate single space
- Dot half space
- Upper and lower case letters
- Space between words
- Position of words in a sentence

V. SPELLING

(see attached suggested list)

VI. ENGLISH

A. Capitalization

- Names, places
- I
- Beginning of sentence
- Beginning of quotes

B. Punctuation

- Period
- Question mark
- Comma
- Exclamation point
- Apostrophe
- Quotation marks
- Hyphen

C. Usage

- Is, are, was, were
- Make, made

- Help, helped
- Go, went, gone

D. Word Forms

- Nouns
- Verbs
- Descriptive words

E. Composition

1. Sentences
    - Recognizing sentences
    - Recognizing statements
    - Recognizing questions
    - Word order
    - Scrambled sentences
    - Sentence completion
    - Writing sentences
2. Paragraphs
    - Indenting
    - Topic sentence
    - Paragraph development

F. Dictionary Skills

- a-b-c order
- Guide words
- Multiple meanings

LEVEL A
SIGHT VOCABULARY

A 1
__ help
__ here
__ go
__ come
__ down

A 2
__ me
__ jump
__ get
__ run
__ look

A 3
__ ball
__ farmer
__ mother
__ away
__ want

A 4
__ see
__ said
__ to
__ hot

A 5
__ did
__ at
__ I
__ that
__ is

A 6
__ find
__ play
__ with
__ in
__ the

A 7
__ no
__ car
__ dog
__ house
__ what

A 8
__ do
__ it
__ a
__ three
__ will

A 9
__ work
__ who
__ up
__ us
__ one

A 10
__ ride
__ my
__ red
__ like
__ little

A 11
__ funny
__ have
__ for
__ how
__ big
__ this

LEVEL B
SIGHT VOCABULARY

B 1
__ back
__ birthday
__ boy
__ cake
__ cat

B 2
__ children
__ chicken
__ coat
__ on
__ saw

B 3
__ need
__ out
__ good
__ there
__ white

B 4
__ your
__ cow
__ day
__ duck
__ farm

B 5
__ find
__ game
__ girl
__ home
__ new

B 6
__ ran
__ after
__ let
__ when
__ them

B 7
__ try
__ yellow
__ horse
__ kitten
__ leg

B 8
__ pig
__ rabbit
__ toy
__ how
__ put

B 9
__ make
__ eat
__ thank
__ then
__ got

B 10
__ walk
__ fast
__ black
__ blue
__ he

B 11
__ where
__ soon
__ they
__ too
__ know

B 12
__ him
__ her
__ please
__ don't
__ she

B 13
__ take
__ so
__ had
__ am
__ are

B 14
__ all
__ pretty
__ was
__ yes
__ came
__ son

B 15
__ January
__ February
__ March
__ April
__ May

B 16
__ June
__ July
__ August
__ September
__ October

B 17
__ November
__ December
__ Sunday
__ Monday
__ Tuesday

B 18
__ Wednesday
__ Thursday
__ Friday
__ Saturday

LEVEL C
SIGHT VOCABULARY

C 1
__ baby
__ beg
__ night
__ shoe
__ were

C 2
__ some
__ show
__ once
__ long

C 3
__ brown
__ going
__ into
__ bird
__ chair

C 4
__ party
__ stick
__ which
__ why
__ give

C 5
__ off
__ any
__ made
__ cut

C 6
__ its
__ hand
__ head
__ picture
__ street

C 7
__ when
__ sleep
__ line
__ must
__ laugh

C 8
__ from
__ buy
__ clean
__ man

C 9
__ rain
__ tree
__ tell
__ wash
__ fine

C 10
__ old
__ could
__ every
__ just
__ as

C 11
__ an
__ morning
__ name
__ well

C 12
__ under
__ our
__ right
__ about
__ four

C 13
__ his
__ may
__ very
__ stop
__ over

C 14
__ of
__ again
__ green
__ has
__ many

C 15
__ wind
__ brother
__ garden
__ window
__ top

C 16
__ bring
__ ask
__ say
__ clean
__ pick

C 17
__ better
__ today
__ apple
__ corn
__ ground

C 18
__ sheep
__ watch
__ both
__ before
__ around

C 19
__ goes
__ pull
__ best
__ small
__ bear

C 20
__ door
__ letter
__ sister
__ water
__ kind

C 21
__ fly
__ start
__ those
__ keep
__ by

C 22
__ would
__ bell
__ fish
__ money
__ snow

C 23
__ far
__ cold
__ six
__ never
__ hurt

C 24
__ or
__ their
__ box
__ flower
__ paper

C 25
__ squirrel
__ does
__ because
__ sit
__ only

C 26
__ light
__ ten
__ eye
__ feet
__ floor

C 27
__ say
__ if
__ always
__ gave
__ much

C 28
__ been
__ use
__ boat
__ father
__ ring

C 29
__ table
__ draw
__ ate
__ live
__ drink

C 30
__ carry
__ bread
__ good-bye
__ five
__ hold

C 31
__ done
__ Christmas
__ grass
__ Santa Claus
__ thing

C 32
__ seed
__ way
__ seven
__ own
__ eight

C 33
__ seed
__ way
__ seven
__ own
__ eight

C 34
__ egg
__ nest
__ sun
__ wood
__ fall

C 35
__ myself
__ grow
__ hot

CREATIVE IDEAS

Sept. 8, 1996

Dear Girls and Boys,

I want to welcome you to first grade. I am so happy to see all of you. I know that we will have a great year. You will all learn a lot and we will have fun!

Love,
Miss Donat

September 8, 1996

Dear Class 1-4 Families,

Welcome to the wonderful world of first grade! To assist you and your child, I have prepared a special subject schedule for ready reference. May I suggest that you label all articles of clothing with your child's name. Please also include names on lunch boxes, lunch bags, school bags and boots!

As far as supplies, I ask that your child come to school with crayons and at least **two** pencils **daily**. Also, **two** marble hardcover notebooks with at least 100 pages will be used for regular homework and a literature log. A large school bag or knapsack will be necessary at all times, as well as two sturdy FRONT pocket folders and a 4x6 index card file box with alphabet separators and accompanying lined index cards of any color.

Corrected classwork will be compiled and sent home on **Mondays only**. Please take time to review your child's encouragement and approval at this crucial juncture.

Lastly, time will be set aside for a snack each day. Please see that your child brings a nutritious daily snack. Also, Show & Tell will generally be first thing every Monday, Wednesday & Friday. I ask you to please monitor your child's selections. This will be explained further.

I thank you in advance and I look forward to a happy, healthy and fulfilling year!

Sincerely,
Patricia Donat

Special Subject Schedule

Miss Donat 1-4	special Class
Monday & Tuesday	Gym — Sneakers must be brought to school or worn on gym days!
Thursday	Music — Bring a smile and your singing voice!
Friday	Library — Books are to be returned on Friday!
Wednesday	A smock (an old, large long sleeved shirt) must be left in school all year!
Daily	Lunch — Don't forget your lunch or money! 12:05-12:50

Also: The Weekly Reader Newspaper will be used this year. is $3.00. Please remit as soon as possible!

Thank You!

Class Tea Notes

Welcome to School & First Grade
Introduce yourself , class mothers & liason
Training Period:

- routines
- attention span
- independent work periods
- listening & following directions
- work habits
- pencil grasp/ writing on lines
- basic vocabulary
- getting along / working together
- testing (Reading placement)
- Weekly work folders

Homework- When it begins and why

- time allotment
- place to work
- parent involvement and attitude
- reasons for: review, continue work habits taught, responsibility

Reading: Assure all children that they will read

- Placement testing for grouping
- Materials
    - Big Books
    - Holt & Macmillan text books
    - Multiple copies of literature trade books
    - new Anthology Series

Handwriting:

- pencil grasp
- letter formation
- posture
- placement of hands
- control of pencil
- spacing of words
- neatness
- copying from board

Process Writing:

- journals
- short books
- emphasis on context of piece with continued growth in
- mechanics
- diversity of topics
- poetry writing
- letter writing, invitations, thank yous

Language:

- listening and following directions
- speaking vocabulary development
- speaking and writing sentences
- telling stories, jokes
- performing simple plays
- show and tell - what days
- SPELLING:
- - starts in late Oct. usually
- - enrichment to follow in January
- - weekly homework teaches planning over time

Math:

- basic operations
- word problems
- graphs
- time, money , measurement
- computer studies weekly
- timed computation drills starting in January
- fractions, probability
- enrichment for all

Science & Social Studies

- seasons
- weather
- birds
- marine life
- experiments
- map skills
- holiday studies
- news
- Health instruction - when-

Other Items:

- Parties
- shoelaces
- birthdays
- SPEECH-
- lunch money
- snacks
- pencils and supplies
- Homework
- Class mothers and parent involvement
- Trips scheduled so far

- bedtime
- T.V.
- Weekly papers
- Extra Help
- absence notes, bus passes, lateness, vacation plans
- emergency dismissal
- after school activities
- clothing- gym, winter etc.

PHILOSOPHY:

-little cutting and pasting
-recess
-movies
-organization, motivation, discipline
-lots of love
-TEACH TO TOP

- enrich all children
- learn to think and be responsible
- establish lasting work habits
- instill a thirst for knowledge
- parent involvement

Conclusion:

- create a happy child
- child skilled in basic subjects
- child who is tolerant and respectful
- child who has a zest for life
- child who is thoughtful and an independent human being

I need:

- your love
- your talents
- your support
- your involvement
- your example
- your structure
- your devotion to their education

Questions?

Fall Plans-1st Quarter Skills

SEPTEMBER:
Handwriting - letters, numerals, pencil grasp, handwriting posture, copying from board, journal writing

Reading - consonant sounds/ text books

- short vowels a and i
- sight word list A
- color words

Math-

- number words (zero- ten)
- number sequences
- inequalities - < = > =
- sets
- number lines

OCTOBER
Handwriting - same as September

Reading -

- short vowels o, e and u
- sight word list A and B
- Big Books, poetry, text books
- Weekly Reader newspaper

Math -

- addition of sets
- domino addition
- number line addition
- addition equalities and inequalities
- ladder addition
- addends and sums

Language -

- periods, question marks
- sentence completion
- writing original sentences
- journals
- a-b-c order
- s, ed and ing endings
- telling and asking sentences
- scrambled sentences
- retelling stories in sequence
- rhyming words
- compound words

Sept. 8, 1996

Dear Parents,

I am delighted to have been chosen to be your child's first grade teacher. In an effort to quickly learn all I can about your child, please write a short or long narrative describing the social, emotional and academic development that has taken place over the last year. Tell me how you see your child, something of your family dynamics, his or her special qualities and your hopes for this all important year!

Please use the accompanying stationery to write your thoughts about your child. These will be saved all year and returned to you in June along with other writings.

Thank you for your help. I look forward to working with all of you and I appreciate your cooperation!

Gratefully,
Patricia Donat

Multi-Purpose Grid For Record Keeping

Miss Donat   Class 1-4

Stephanie											
Christopher											
Lawrence											
Sean											
Nathaniel											
Avery											
Alexa											
David											
Sean											
Alyssa											
Sahil											
Harrison											
Laurie											
Gina											
Meaghan											
Noreen											
Jamie											
Suzanne											
Jon											
Henry											
Alexandra											

Weekly Report

Name: Lawrence **Date:**

	Excellent	Very Good	Good	Satisfactory	Improving	Needs Improvement
Creative Writing		X				
Spelling	X					
Handwriting	X					
Phonics	X					
Speaking Vocabulary	X					
Reading Comprehension	X					
Math Skills		X				
Work Completion			X			
Listening	X					
Effort	X					
Behavior		X				

Lawrence continues to put his heart and soul into everything he does. He is so aware of everything in his environment. Lawrence has opinions and he can reason and infer with a maturity well beyond his years. It is a continuing delight to have Lawrence in class this year! Sure wish time was not flying by for me! Lawrence is beyond special! He is an example to all who know him!

Weekly Report

Name: Sean **Date:**

	Excellent	Very Good	Good	Satisfactory	Improving	Needs Improvement
Creative Writing	X					
Spelling	X					
Handwriting	X					
Phonics	X					
Speaking Vocabulary	X					
Reading Comprehension	X					
Math Skills	X					
Work Completion	X					
Listening	X					
Effort	X					
Behavior	X					

Sean is just the most wonderful child a teacher could ever possibly know. He is perfect in every way. Sean has **fantastic manners and a sense of humility that few adults have. He has terrific poise and an unbelievable** sense of tact. I truly hope that Sean will always have educational experiences that will further enhance his skills **and bring him continued joy in learning! He is an outstanding child by all measurements!**

Weekly Reading Homework
Books I Read This Week
(one book per day)

	Date	Book Title
Monday		
Tuesday		
Wednesday		
Thursday		

Weekly Reading Homework
Books I Read This Week
(one book per day)

	Date	Book Title
Monday		
Tuesday		
Wednesday		
Thursday		

Sept. 14, 1996

Dear ______________________________,

Thank you for doing such a great job with your Kindergarten class last year. It is clearly evident that you put forth a concerted effort to cover the Kindergarten curriculum both horizontally and vertically, while attempting to meet the varying individual needs each child brings to the learning environment.

The children I received have been exposed to good training and each has amassed usable readiness skills. Now it is up to me to add on to the foundation you have begun before building a sturdy first floor!

I commend you for your creativity, stamina, your patience, understanding, your talents and your love of this "bud-like" age group! May continued success, good health and happiness be yours in the future!

Fondly,
Patricia Donat

PARENT GUIDELINES
SEPTEMBER

- Establish a homework routine - (time & place)
- Set aside time daily to read to your child
- Set bedtime no later than 8P.M. on school nights
- Praise weekly work that is brought home on Mondays
- Provide meaningful family experiences
- Consciously and purposefully build speaking vocabulary
- Talk to and with your child
- Limit T. V. viewing, video and computer games
- Monitor movie selections
- Don't over-program your youngster with after school activities and other weekly commitments

Oct. 5, 1996

Dear Parents,

As your child's teacher, I am truly concerned with the enormity of the task we have as guiders of the young.

Therefore in my search for answers, I'd like to know your thinking on the questions enclosed.

I strongly feel that by working together we can explore avenues of discussion on topics relating to all of us.

I look forward to your quick responses and I thank you for your time, your energy and your love. Together we can surely help all of our children become everything they can be!

Sincerely,
Patricia Donat

Name______________________________

Questionnaire

1. What things frustrate or concern you most about being a parent?

2. What pressures from society impinge upon your ability to handle your role as a parent?

3. What are your goals for your children?

4. Besides academics, how can the school assist you in the overall development of your child?

5. What do you feel is the most important thing you can do in guiding your child to become an adult?

6. Would you be interested in spending time with me in an informal way to just talk about and share concerns regarding the parenting of all children?

   [ ] YES [ ] NO

FIRST MARKING PERIOD GUIDE

1. Most children are somewhere between the readiness and emergent learner. Therefore, except in isolated cases and only in rare subjects, such as (handwriting) could one or should one expect a grade of "E". Realistically, very few children could be considered achieving in an excellent manner on a daily basis. Naturally, there are exceptions. Be wise and "talk up" "S" and "G" grades! Older siblings do not need to comment negatively on first grade marks!!!

2. Cursive writing is NOT taught in first grade, thus the use of the *.

3. Math problem solving and Spelling and Computer Literacy will NOT be graded this quarter.

4. Clearly all children are trying their best. Consider the Social and Work habits box as your focal point of interest. These grades hold the key to real academic success. The child who is organized, motivated, serious, mature and willing to take direction will soar past his or her classmates. Intelligence is NOT the crucial variable here. An over achiever can often surpass the bulk of his classmates due to sheer drive and determination.

5. Remember that earned praise and steady encouragement from home and school build the kind of confidence that transforms a child into a student!

6. Make report card days satisfying and thought-inducing experiences that ultimately teach children to focus on self-improvement, a skill that involves us all!!!

January, 1997

Dear Parents,

Now that we have completed half the year, I would like to discuss ways you can help your child.

In order to continue progressing, I must ask each of you to redouble your efforts in the following areas.

Please be sure to assist, guide and check homework daily. It will be getting much harder. Drill spelling words and especially enrichment words for a test every Friday. Start practicing number facts to 18, such as 6 + 9 = 15, 18 - 9 = 9. Using fingers over ten is very difficult. These facts must be memorized. Make or buy flashcards which present <u>both</u> plus and minus facts. We have a timed drill test daily.

Above all, read daily with your child, and mark the weekly sheet in the homework book. This will continue till June. Take turns reading to each other. Reading is a lifetime skill which must be practiced and enjoyed.

Continue to praise your child's efforts. First grade is very hard. Remember, the more you work with your child, the better he or she will be for it. I need your help to insure that our goals will be reached. Thank you in advance!

Sincerely,
Patricia Donat

March, 1997

Dear Parents,

Now that the school - wide P.A.R.P. program has begun, I would like these types of reading incentives to continue. Because of the special efforts to provide motivating activities, the children have been discovering books and perfecting their reading skills at the same time.

My next step is to have each child share a favorite book by reading it to our class. Please help your child choose a suitable book that he or she feels comfortable reading (and one not overly long). We'll steer them in the right direction. They may borrow a book from the class library if they choose. Each child will have their time to shine as the official "Reader of the Day"! This activity will be followed by a special pre-arranged visit to read to the class of the Kindergarten teacher of their choice. This ego booster pays dividends in self confidence, pride and maturity that are lasting, while serving to renew an initally special ans hopefully meaningful relationship. A positive message of hope is also sent to nervous Kindergarten children about the joys of learning to read in first grade!

I'll send home a copy of the schedule so you'll know when your child will read so that you can allow for adequate time to practice. Again, I thank you for all your help and cooperation.

Yours truly,
Miss Donat

March 9, 1998

Dear Parents,

Just a note to inform you of upcoming events in the life and times of Class 1-4. It seems to me that our year together is beginning to slide by rather quickly.

You presently have before you a packet on P.A.R.P. (Parents As Reading Partners). This is nothing new for our class, as daily reading is a standard assignment since January. Do continue to write the title of the book or chapter read daily on the back inside cover of your child's homework book. Also, initial the enclosed calender daily so that your child gets credit for your combined involvement in P.A.R.P. I expect 100% participation!!!

Also, I have tentatively scheduled a combined Passover/Easter party for Tuesday, April 7 at about 2:15. At that time we will learn how Mrs. __________ makes her chocolate delights. We'll also have the traditional goodies, hide some matzah and eggs and play a game. All are welcome to attend!

My next Parenting meeting will be held on Wed., March 18 at 2:15. We will be discussing CHILDREN'S NEEDS VS.

WANTS! We will also continue discussing the february topic of Parental Responsibilities re: Academics! Coffee will be served. Hope to see you then!

Thanks to all the parents who have come forth to read to Class 1-4. I hope you found the experience a pleasant one. You have helped broaden our sights. There is still time to sign up. Furthermore, siblings of Class 1-4 will be invited to sign up to read as well. watch for invitations to come home with your child.

Lastly, our first graders are to begin preparing a book to read to the class as part of my "READER OF THE DAY" Program. any book your child likes will be fine. Following their presentation, each child will bew allowed to visit their kindergarten class. This is usually an unbelievable confidence builder enjoyed by all! Your help with this assignment will be greatly appreciated. A "Reader of the Day" calender will be forthcoming!

Thank you for your kind attention and cooperation!

Yours truly,
Miss Donat

March, 1998

Dear Girls & Boys,

Please begin to think of a very favorite book that you would enjoy reading to our class. Each of you will have a turn to be "READER OF THE DAY" during the month of May. The book may be on any topic, fiction or non-fiction.

Practice reading your book and I know that you will feel special when your turn comes. I look forward to hearing each of your selections! I continue to be very proud of your efforts in class and at home!

Love,
Miss Donat

April, 1998

Dear Parents,

Now that the third quarter of this school year has ended, I want to express to you how proud and delighted I am with the progress "our" children have made.

We are working on more advanced skills in every area. Homework, continues to require your help as an overseer or it will cease to be a worthwhile component of our program. In the area of more complex math concepts you should begin to see the impact of accurate computational skills and the ability to read directions. Reading, writing and spelling continue to be the core of the Language Arts program. Happily, many of your children have become prolific writers thanks to the Process Writing Program started in September. "I don't know what to write about.", is a statement hardly, but happily ever heard anymore. We are collecting all writing projects, which will be discussed and presented to you on Portfolio Day!!! DON'T MISS IT !!!

Please redouble your efforts in all areas, so that productive learning will continue to take place even though spring has actually arrived!

Needless to say, I am truly impressed and encouraged by the growth each child has made. They are enthusiastic, bright and willing to take on any academic challenge. Thus, we will forge ahead in all areas despite spring fever.

In order to make the precious time we have together as exciting and fulfilling as possible, I will soon be sending you a schedule of end-of-the-year events, which I hope will close our super experience on a high note!

Thank you all for your boundless energy, your devotion to Class 1-4 and especially for the respect, love and support you have so freely given me.

"Our" children are wonderful and so are you!

Yours truly,
Patricia Donat

4TH QUARTER SKILLS

LANGUAGE

- completing stories
- book reports
- writing science reports
- poetry
- grammar, pronouns, adjectives
- endings (er, ly, est, ness, able, tion, sion)
- doubling consonants (stop-stopping)
- dropping final "e" (love-loving)
- more syllables & a-b-c order
- dictionary work (guide words, definitions)

READING

- Big Book Fairy Tale classics
- Reading and acting out plays
- Complete Grade 1 Treasury of Literature for most children
- Simple chapter books for some children

MATH

- telling time(hours, half hours, and 5 minute intervals

- money (penny, nickel, dime, quarter, half dollar, dollar
- adding coins/making change
- fractional parts(halves, thirds, fourths)
- fractions of sets (half of 8=?)
- harder word problems
- writing numerals to the thousands
- multiplication of sets
- multiplication on the number line
- relating multiplication to addition
- measurement
- geometric shapes
- carrying and borrowing
- place value & expanded notation to the hundreds
- numeral dictation

April 20, 1998

Dear Parents,

I truly cannot believe that this wonderful year is rapidly barreling toward its end at seemingly breakneck speed!

You have all worked hard and studied for timed tests, spelling quizzes and helped to guide the learning process by reading and supervising homework daily, attending parenting meetings, insisting on loving discipline and mostly by cooperating with the tenets of my educational philosophy which hopefully by now you have seen the merits of firsthand! Teaching to the top, setting high personal goals, being organized, motivating, loving and skill oriented is achieved only through hard work, including daily drill, modeling, praise and personal example!

It is fondly hoped that you will continue the above over the summer and that you will all enjoy the activities I have prepared for Class 1-4. Times and dates may have to be changed or events eliminated for one reason or another. Parent volunteers may also be necessary. This will be noted as the case may be.

Please save these sheets to help remind you and your child of our proposed schedule! Thank you again!

Yours truly,
Patricia Donat

CLASS 1-4

ENDING ACTIVITIES

Fri., Apr. 24th	Parenting Mtg. "Parental Potpourri" - 8:15 - 9
Fri., May 1st	T-Shirt Day!
Tues., May 5th	Parent Mtg. on 2nd Grade! 12:15 - 1:15 P.M.
Thurs., May 8th	PICNIC DAY! - Have lunch in courtyard with Miss Donat! (weather permitting)
Fri., May 16th	BOWLING DAY! - Enjoy a class outing including dinner. Parents must supervise. Moreinfo. to come.
Tues., May 20th	FIELD DAY! - Gym activity for K-2! Wear your team color!
Thurs., May 22nd	HOFSTRA PLAYHOUSE - "Amelia Bedelia"
Fri., May 23rd	CRAZY MIXED-UP DAY! - Wear outfits, shoes, bows, socks etc. that don't match. Mixed up schedule too!

Thurs., May 29th	PERFORMING DAY! - All parents are encouraged to come and be entertained by Class 1-4, as we become authors, actors, singers and sharers of knowledge! The performance will be taped. No pre-schoolers please! Refreshments will be served 12:30 - 3:00 (approx.)
Tues., June 3rd	T-SHIRT DAY! - Wear your favorite & most interesting shirt to school!
Mon., June 9th	PICNIC DAY #2 - Have your lunch with Miss Donat in the courtyard!
Wed., June 11th	TRIP TO SUFFOLK CTY. FARM - Guided tour and lesson included!
Fri., June 13th	STUFFED ANIMAL DAY!- Bring your favorite pal to school. Be able to tell about your pal!
Wed., June 18th	ERASER DAY! - Bring an accurate count of the eraser collection you have won as prizes this year!

Thurs., June 19th	PORTFOLIO DAY! - 2:00 Parents may come to see, admire and collect all the creative work amassed this year! Bravo!!!
Fri., June 20th	"ME" DAY !- Prepare a card trick, magic, a dance, a gymnastics act, a karate demonstration etc. to share with classmates! Ice cream Sundae Class Party at 2:00!
Mon., June 23rd	AUTOGRAPH DAYS! - We will collect and share auto-graphs over the next 3 days. Books will be provided!
Tues., June 24th	TOY DAY! - Bring your favorite toy to share!
Wed., June 25th	HAT DAY! - Wear your favorite specialty hat. It could be made!

ENRICHMENT SPELLING LIST
GRADE 1

please
summer
teacher
around
because
morning
before
excitement
grade
friend
found
brother
again
elementary
should
Sunday
Monday
Tuesday
Wednesday
Thursday
Friday
Saturday
January
February
March
April
May
ocean

June
July
August
September
October
November
December
another
always
picture
lunch
second
watch
north
without
airplane
outside
anything
sister
cross
tonight
afraid
butterfly
swimming
grandma
finally
brought
Indian

monkey
already
baseball
following
hundred
reading
window
spelling
winter
nothing
enough
woman
person
south
country
answer
wonderful
river
television
straight
bicycle
people
grocery
vacation
department
difficult
carefully
performing

champion
envelope
hospital
dangerous
important
America
Africa
Europe
mountain
Asia
Australia
Antarctica
directions
east
west
Chestnut
Hill
New York
Dix Hills
Melville
Easter
Passover
spring
primary
challenge
Atlantic
Pacific
playbill

SPEAKING VOCABULARY
CLASS 1-4
97-98

spatula
wick
bait
blade
amphibians
mini
prey
swamp
trophy
vertical
solar system
lungs
veins
bark
huge
cotton
zoom
arachnid
invisible
solid
drowsy
enormous
vowel
curtain
navigator
lagoon
carve
photograph
display

cone
basement
scales(fish)
weapon
mammal
tricycle
digit
pond
states
lungs
planets
delicate
telescope
tripod
gigantic
apron
encyclopedia
liquor
state
gas
envious
gourds
consonant
drapes
bolt
deserted
spice
Manhattan
harmonica

funnel
cellar
liquid
gills
instinct
triplets
tornado
fossil
badger
phonics
center
migrate
characters
herbivore
vine
island
dictionary
alcohol
country
expand
scorched
rotten
tangle
blinds
carpenter
spade
pebbles
stories/floors
patch

wax
minnow
puck
nocturnal
camouflage
triangle
twister
volcano
horizontal
totem pole
energy
hibernate
chain
carnivore
rise
axis
vibrate
indelible
district
retract
surrounded
eagle
threading
voyage
meteor
soil
albino
solar panel
biscuit

ban
compass
toss
friction
canine
mold
dull
series
hinge
assassinated
liberty
similarities
surveyor
saturate
energy
primary
plantation
monument
albino
paragraph
splendiferous

placemat
profile
universal
Broadway
peninsula
reins
pantomime
wigwam
mallet
lair
fact
differences
scenery
dessert
disintegrate
permanent
autograph
dedication
evaporate
summary
retire

copper
silhouette
explorer
broad
autumn
saddle
charades
wampum
lark
allegiance
fiction
comparing
slavery
orbit
categories
foe
autobiography
illustrator
estimate
virus
laminate

mercury
studio
collection
origami
molar
harness
decay
powwow
seminar
pledge
character
created
honest
billiards
monocle
notion
colonies
publisher
germ
splendid
doe

CHALLENGE OF CHAMPIONS
(QUESTIONS FOR TEAMS)

1. Give an example of a liquid.
2. What category do lizards belong to?
3. In the Pledge, which word means freedom?
4. What word describes an animal's ability to hide itself from danger?
5. What word names a lion's home?
6. Spell the word automobile!
7. What name is given to any animal taken for food by another animal?
8. What word means to stop working at a paying job?
9. What do we call a place where scientists perform experiments?
10. Give an example of a gas?
11. How can we describe animals that are no longer alive?
12. Name a country north of the U.S.
13. Name a country south of the U.S.
14. Name a three digit number with no tens.
15. What animal is called a buck?
16. What does glimmer mean?
17. What does fragile mean?
18. Pumpkins grow on ________?
19. What happens to our courtyard on very heavy rainy days?
20. What do birds do every fall?
21. What is a book of maps called?
22. Who studies dinosaurs?

23. What does the word pledge mean?
24. What is the following an example of?
    2tens 4ones = 20 + 4 = 24
25. Name an animal that hibernates?
26. What verb describes how a snake moves?
27. What does contagious mean?
28. What word means to disappear?
29. Rubbing two solids together creates something called ________?
30. Someone's signature is also called an __________.
31. What word refers to the sun?
32. The earth spins on what?
33. Spiders belong to which animal category?
34. Which animal group can be described as warm-blooded?
35. What word describes the hair around a lion?
36. What is the name given to a female fox?
37. What word describes the north to south movement?
38. What name describes animals who hunt at night?
39. What is the sum of 6 and 8?
40. What word means that something MUST be done?
41. What animal category do frogs belong to?
42. What name is given to the metal bar which supports a seesaw?
43. Which word describes the east to west movement?
44. Where do fruit trees grow?
45. What is the word "can't" an example of?
46. What word in the Pledge means fairness?

47. What is the name given to the Earth's path around the sun?
48. What animal category do butterflies belong to?
49. What piece of land do we live on?
50. What makes Manhattan an island?
51. What does surrounded mean?
52. What light is the Statue of Liberty holding?
53. In the number sentence 12 = 3 + 9, what do we call the 3?
54. What makes a bird, a bird?
55. What do we call an animal's inherited behavior?
56. What do we call a person who runs for office?
57. What is the name given to a female deer?
58. What are meat-eating animals called?
59. What do mirrors show you?
60. Mr. is an example of what?
61. What do you call an event that cannot be explained?
62. What verb describes the spinning of the earth?
63. What do we call an exploding mountain?
64. What ocean is closest to New York?
65. How many states do we have in America?
66. What continent do we live on?
67. How many colonies were part of our country in the early days?
68. Who was our first president?
69. What was the name of the War between the States?
70. What was Lincoln most famous for?
71. What word describes how Lincoln was killed?
72. How many planets are there?
73. Which planet is closest to the sun?

74. Which ocean is near California?
75. Who was our third president?
76. Which early president was a farmer?
77. Which number was given to Lincoln's presidency?
78. Which river runs through New York?
79. Which river almost cuts the U.S. in half?
80. Name a continent country?
81. What is the earth mostly made of?
82. What do a group of sentences make up?
83. What 3 things usually make mammals fit their category?
84. In the Pledge which word refers to our form of government?
85. What 5 syllable word is found in the Pledge of Allegiance?
86. What else is the earth doing while it is spinning?

SUMMER DICTIONARY LIST

Find the definition of each word below and add the index card to your Vocabulary Box in a-b-c order! GOOD LUCK!

1. amphibian	2. prey	3. vertical
4. veins	5. huge	6. arachnid
7. invisible	8. drowsy	9. enormous
10. vowel	11. weapon	12. tripod
13. encyclopedia	14. envious	15. consonant
16. instinct	17. migrate	18. herbivore
19. expand	20. Contract	21. scorched

NAME____________________ DATE__________

FIRST GRADE EVALUATION

1. Put these school subjects in the order of MOST enjoyed to LEAST enjoyed by numbering them 1,2,3,4 up to 11!

_____reading _____math _____spelling
_____handwriting _____science _____language
_____story writing _____phonics_____vocabulary
_____health _____social studies

2. Do the same for your special subject classes!

_____library _____art _____music
_____gym _____projects

3. Who is your favorite special teacher?

_____Mrs. __________ _____Mr. __________
_____Mrs. __________ _____Mr. __________
_____Mrs. __________ _____Mr. __________
_____Mrs. __________ _____Mr. __________
_____Mrs. __________

4. Who is your favorite lunch aide?

_____Mrs. __________ _____Mr. __________
_____Mrs. __________ _____Mr. __________

5. Which teacher do you think you would like for second grade?

_____Mrs. __________ _____Mr. __________
_____Mrs. __________ _____Mr. __________

6. What do you think about the way Miss Donat teaches? Explain!

____

____

____

7. What is the best thing about Miss Donat or What does she maybe do better than other teachers?

____

____

____

____

8. What was your most favorite trip?

____

9. What was your most favorite activity or project?

____

10. What is the most important thing you learned this year?

____

____

____

____

11. Do you think you had too much homework this year?

____

____

____

____

12. Who was your best friend in class this year?

____

13. How do you feel about school ending this week?

____

____

____

14. What will you remember most about first grade?

15. Is there anything you think Miss Donat could do to improve her teaching and your learning?

16. What are your summer plans?

17. Write an ending to describe first grade!

VOCABULARY DEVELOPMENT

Excerpted from letter to the Superintendent from Pat Donat, Teacher

"One area of special interest to parents must definitely be the development of language. Our language is the means by which we communicate. To express ideas, and to receive likewise in return, is one area of profound importance. Acquiring effective and precise language can mean the difference between life and death, happiness or despair, or even the entrance into the university or job of choice. A high degree of language proficiency separates us from lower forms of animal life and allows us to consider ourselves educated. Our language is an integral part of what makes us human. It is a fundamental need of all of us to be able to communicate our needs, feelings, and desires."

"Since the teaching of reading is intrinsically intertwined with language development, it behooves us all to look upon the elements of language that much be developed over time."

"One such element is the emerging and the fine tuning of vocabulary. Words, words, words! Each word a toddler learns represents the beginnings of an idea, a thought, a bit of information. From birth to pre-school, babies and toddlers hear and begin to reproduce words. Those words name concrete things. This is how it starts and this is when pre-schoolers need to be systematically taught the names of things in their world. Organized by categories, children can learn the terms for items of clothing, body parts, foods, toys, furniture, tools, pets, kitchen equipment, and the like. Trips to the supermarket are invaluable. All stores are veritable classrooms waiting to be discovered. The names of everything in our world can be found there!"

"How can children learn to express ideas when they have a limited number of words at their disposal? Abstract ideas need explicit explanation. Children cannot be taught the multitude of skills necessary to read without first acquiring an abundant and rich vocabulary. Spoken and written language depend on vocabulary. Words are fascinating. Many have multiple meanings conveying different ideas depending on the context. Words can suggest sounds, i.e. grunt, groan, thump. Words describe feelings, i.e. frustrated, blue, determined. Words add a richness and a necessary order to our lives."

"All too often, however, as parents we are caught up in the routines of life and miss those chances to really aid in our children's academic growth. We take for granted that children know the meaning of simple things. We set out our youngster's clothes, not realizing that he or she cannot distinguish between a tee shirt, a polo shirt, a denim, or a sweatshirt, or a sweater, not to mention a turtle-neck shirt! They don't know striped from plaid or solid, or even what tie-dyed shirts are like. These seemingly simple decisions involving choice become invaluable learning experiences for young children, ones that will insure a systematic development – 'environmental vocabulary.'"

"Teachers have witnessed a decline in the level of vocabulary development in children entering school over the last 15 years. The emergence of computers and video games, coupled with T.V. and movies, have done little or nothing to enhance learning in the area of vocabulary. Reading, discussions, and family excursions have taken a back-seat to the aforementioned activities. Vocabulary suffers as a result, or this delicate process must be built in and enriched by human contact. Language is a human phenomenon. Words and their meanings are a joy!"

"To know the names of things in our world is to better understand who we are, what we are, and where we are going – the vocabulary process."

Pat Donat,
Teacher